ALL GOD'S CHILDREN
AND BLUE SUEDE SHOES

TURNING POINT Christian Worldview Series
Marvin Olasky, General Editor

ALL GOD'S CHILDREN AND BLUE SUEDE SHOES

*Christians &
Popular Culture*

Kenneth A. Myers

CROSSWAY BOOKS • WHEATON, ILLINOIS
A DIVISION OF GOOD NEWS PUBLISHERS

All God's Children and Blue Suede Shoes.

Copyright © 1989 by Kenneth A. Myers.

Published by Crossway Books, a division of
Good News Publishers, Wheaton, Illinois 60187.

 Published in association with the
Fieldstead Institute
P.O. Box 19061,
Irvine, California 92713

Cover photo: Comstock, Inc.

First printing, 1989

Printed in the United States of America

Unless otherwise noted, all Bible quotations are taken from *Holy
Bible: New International Version*, copyright © 1978 by the New
York International Bible Society. Used by permission of Zondervan
Bible Publishers.

Library of Congress Catalog Card Number 89-50321

ISBN 0-89107-538-0

15	14	13	12	11	10	09	08	07	06	05	04	03	02	01
23	22	21	20	19	18	17	16	15	14	13	12	11	10	

For Susannah and Jonathan,
who are even more fun than
"The Rockford Files"

TABLE OF

CONTENTS

ACKNOWLEDGMENTS

Thanks to William M. Brailsford for his camaraderie in discussing words and ideas, to David Coffin for theological wisdom, to John Muether for providing me with reference material I was too lazy to find myself, to my editor Marvin Olasky for his patience, and to my wife, Kate, who was my faithful coach and companion as I went through the labor of giving birth to this book.

IMMEDIATELY YOURS

THE PLAGUE OF TERMINAL TRENDINESS

Let's begin by establishing your Pop Culture Quotient (PCQ). First, how many entertainment appliances are in your house? Count all the radios, televisions, VCRs, video cameras, cable-TV descrambler boxes, television antenna controllers, CD players, cassette decks, boom boxes, turntables, graphic equalizers, receivers, and computer game units. (Unless you find some very strange things amusing, don't include microwave ovens or blenders.) If you're of a certain age, you may have a lava-lamp in the attic. Count that too. If it's still in your living room, count it twice.

Now count up the number of magazines you subscribe to or read regularly, excluding academic journals founded before 1958 and denominational publications. Count *People, Us, Self,* and all supermarket tabloids twice. Count *TV Guide* three times if you actually *read* it. Count *Sports Illustrated* four times if you ordered it just to get the swimsuit issue. (Also talk to your pastor.) If you get *Sports Illustrated* and throw away the swimsuit issue *without* reading it, subtract three from your total. Count *Spy* twice if you laugh at it, three times if you read it regularly and don't laugh at all. Subtract three if you live within 300 miles of New York City and you've never heard of *Spy.*

Finally, calculate how many books you've read in the last ninety days that were romance novels, detective novels, horror novels, thrillers, westerns, or any bestseller not by Allan Bloom or Stephen Hawking.

Now add up the total for all three categories. Note that the PCQ does not attempt to calculate how much your life is actually *influenced* by the popular culture around you, but simply how many *conduits* of popular culture to which you are connected.

If you scored less than 10, your life is semimonastic, and you won't really enjoy or need to read this book. If you scored between 10 and 20, you probably have an average level of contact with popular culture, which means a much higher level than your parents and their parents had. If you scored between 20 and 35, you probably have a high susceptibility to terminal trendiness and chronic couch potatoism and ought to have your cholesterol level checked. If your score was over 35, you should consider checking into the Faith Popcorn Clinic for the Severely Overacculturated or a similar institution. But first, read this book.

LIVING IN THE MATERIAL WORLD

Every generation of Christians faces unique challenges. The first-century Church had Caesar's lions and the Colosseum. Christians a few hundred years later, following the conversion of Constantine, enjoyed more liberty for exercising their faith, but faced the terror of Visigoth, Ostrogoth, and Bulgar invaders. Still later the peril of plague swept through Europe and, unlike certain Biblical pestilences, showed no discrimination between the faithful and the wicked. The sixteenth century brought the renaissance of Biblical truth in the Protestant Reformation, but it also brought religious wars and persecution by competing churches.

It might seem an extreme assertion at first, but I believe that *the challenge of living with popular culture* may well be as serious for modern Christians as persecution and plagues were for the saints of earlier centuries. Being thrown to the lions or living in the shadow of gruesome death are fairly straightforward if unattractive threats. Enemies that come loudly and visibly are usually much easier to fight than those that are undetectable. Physical affliction (even to the point of death) for the sake of Christ is a heavy cross, but at least it can be readily recognized at the time as a trial of faith. But the erosion of character, the spoiling of innocent pleasures, and the cheapening of life itself that often accompany modern popular culture can occur so subtly that we believe nothing has happened.

Christian concern about popular culture should be as much about the sensibilities it encourages as about its content. This book focuses on those sensibilities. Many other studies look at the content of rock 'n' roll lyrics, of television programs, of movies, and of popular fiction. (Some of these are listed in the Bibliography, which I have made more extensive than the focus of this book.) In this study, I have tried to make the case that popular culture's greatest influence is in the way it shapes *how* we think and feel (more than *what* we think and feel) and how we think and feel about thinking and feeling.

This is not a book that calls for monasticism or asceticism. There was a time in my life when I believed that Christian obedience required escape from modern culture. That was also a time when I was very far from Christian orthodoxy, being intoxicated by mysticism from the East and obscure teachings that had virtually nothing to do with Christian discipleship as presented by Christ's disciples.

Popular culture, like the meat offered to idols in 1 Corinthians 10, is a part of the created order, part of the earth that is the Lord's, and thus something capable of bringing innocent pleasure to believers. But not everything that is permissible is constructive. That is the main theme of this book.

Modern American popular culture presents many opportunites for innocent pleasures, but its principal attributes are, I believe, obstacles to enjoying the best of human experience. Popular culture is in many ways a very trivial matter. Some readers may balk at taking it so seriously. But its triviality, while making it seem innocuous, also enables it to be extremely pervasive, and that is its most toxic quality. It unobtrusively provides the backdrop, scenery, costumes, minor characters, script, and background noise of much of our lives. When we arrive, the stage is already set, the lyrics and music written, our lines and our movements already determined. Popular culture has the power to set the pace, the agenda, and the priorities for much of our social and our spiritual existence, without our explicit consent. It requires a great effort not to be mastered by it.

THE INSTANT SELF

Part of the attractiveness of popular culture is that so much can be ours immediately. Nothing need get in the way of our enjoying its offerings. Time is no obstacle: with VCRs and the practice of time-shifting, we can watch a program scheduled for 3:00 A.M. during breakfast. Thanks to cable television, news, weather, sports, movies, music, and even shopping are all instantly available. Talent or experience is not a prerequisite. One need not take classes in music appreciation to listen to the latest release from Madonna.

By contrast, folk art and high art are mediated by certain conventions that require more discipline, more familiarity with and submission to the tradition in which they stand. A jazz standard (I consider jazz a hybrid of folk and high culture rather than popular culture) such as "Autumn Leaves" performed by trumpeter Wynton Marsalis is more demanding than whatever Casey Kasem is hyping this week, in part because the many previous renditions of the ballad form a canon of sorts that Marsalis is aware of and responding to.

Popular culture, on the other hand, specializes in instant gratification. But like most instant things, it may spoil your taste for something better.

There are, of course, occasions when something instant is a useful option. When I was in college, I began the habit of coffee-drinking by partaking of a fluid labeled "coffee" that was dispensed out of a machine in a grimy room in the building where I had my first class of the day. At 7:30 A.M., after a late night of study, I was more interested in the drink's stimulative capacities than in a gourmet experience. After a few weeks of the stuff, I was offered some freshly ground, freshly brewed coffee — in other words, some *real* coffee. It took some getting used to, since it was so different from that thin, bitter liquid I had been sipping out of those cardboard cups on campus. For a long time after that, I actually preferred instant coffee to the brewed variety. Only after I weaned myself off the instant could I realize what I had been missing.

It is possible to develop a taste for instant everything. One could eat instant, drink instant, read instant, think instant, hear instant, love instant, and pray instant. One of the concerns of this book is that popular culture encourages a mood of expecting everything to be immediate, a mood that deters greater depth and breadth in other areas of our lives, including our understanding of Christianity and our experience of obedient faith.

I did not set out simply to condemn popular culture, but to understand it, and that is the spirit in which I think this book can best be read. I will be disappointed to learn of readers who simply jumped to my conclusions, not because I worked so hard at getting to them myself and want some company, but because I want my readers, like the Bereans, to be fully persuaded that what I am presenting is true. In reading books and in making arguments, the point is not to change the world, but to understand it. Otherwise we will never know what it is that may need changing, nor how change can be pursued in a way that shows proper love to God and to our neighbors. My interest in culture is finally an interest in understanding how to be obedient to God and to glorify Him. Without thoughtful and loving obedience, all our allegedly prophetic stands against the shortcomings of our culture are worse than clanging cymbals.

Since my goal is first to understand popular culture, I will have to begin with some definitions. Once I have established an idea of what is meant by culture, I will then look at some Biblical teaching that relates to that complex topic. Then I will focus on popular culture, what distinguishes it from culture as such, what its historical origins are, some of the history of critical thinking on popular culture, and how the war between popular culture and high culture effectively ended in the 1960s. Finally, I will look at some of the characteristics of popular culture as expressed by its dominant *idiom*, rock 'n' roll, and mediated by its dominant *medium*, television. Television and rock 'n' roll are the most significant forces in shaping popular culture and the culture at large. They both communicate in an immediate, emotional form. Their style is not only the epitome of the style of popular culture, it is the essence of the spirit of our age. The marriage of the two in music videos, especially in the phenomenon of the cable channels that play nonstop videos, is a perfect marriage, if not one made in Heaven.

I am more concerned here with how popular culture affects the way people perceive reality than with how social structures exercise power. There is a great deal of wisdom in Marshall McLuhan's observation that "the medium is the message." The forms of our popular culture may well have a more significant effect on our perceptions than the content. This is why I do not believe that much would be improved if, all other things being equal, Christians could somehow take over all of the instruments of popular culture, even if they were very talented and orthodox Christians.

Rather than starting our own TV networks, movie production companies, or imitations of *People*, we would do much better to make the church a living example of alternatives to the methods and messages of popular culture. Virtually all cultural institutions, from literature professors at Ivy League schools to producers of soap operas to the loudest heavy metal bands, are equally bereft of points of perspective for their activities. In such a time, the church *could* be a community displaying, in its corporate life and in the lives of its members, a *culture of transcendence*. This would not mean escaping from the world. It *would* require refusing to conform to its ways, not only when they are evil, but when they are not beneficial or constructive (see 1 Corinthians 10:23ff.). I hope this book provides some wisdom to encourage the discernment necessary for such a worthy task.

OF THE WORLD, BUT NOT IN THE WORLD

A family moves to a new city. The decision to move was made for financial reasons, the father believing there were much greater opportunities for prosperity in the new location. After they arrive, they discover that the cultural surroundings of their new home are fraught with obstacles for their family's spiritual well-being. While the economic opportunities are there, the city turns out to be a moral cesspool. Unwilling or unable to relocate, the family suffers horribly, resulting in the death of the mother, the loss of their home as they flee in terror of physical violence, and, eventually sexual sin between daughters and father.

This could be the outline for a sweeps-week miniseries on one of the networks, but this scenario is actually one of the earliest recorded instances of the effects of a culture on the lives of individuals and families. It is, of course, the story of Lot and his family.

We are not told Lot's thoughts about the culture that destroyed his family. We do not know if he reflected on his earlier decision to move to the cities of the plain, while his Uncle Abram pitched his tents near the great trees of Mamre. While the Genesis account (chapter 19) says very little about Lot's spiritual life, the Apostle Peter tells us that Lot was "a righteous man, who was distressed by the filthy lives of lawless men (for that righteous man, living among them day after day, was tormented in his righteous soul by the lawless deeds he saw and heard)" (2 Peter 2:7ff.).

There are many Christians in the twentieth century who sometimes feel as if they have settled in Sodom. A culture that once was dominated by Christian values is now one of the greatest spiritual challenges for American Christians. Once decency and order seemed to characterize the lives of individuals and communities. The institutions they created and the traditions they respected seemed to make American culture more hospitable to Christianity than any culture in history. American society was regarded as a "Christian society."

Earlier generations of Christians were concerned about "worldliness," and whatever that meant, it was seen as an aberration in American culture, not its essence. But today most Christians regard their culture itself as an implacable enemy, a constant threat to their own sanctity and to the stability and faith of their families.

More specifically, what is called "popular culture" has been troubling to parents, teachers, pastors, and counselors for generations. The effects of television, movies, popular music, fiction, fashion, and other aspects of popular culture have been debated intensely, if not always intelligently. Much of the attention has been focused on the content of popular culture, especially material that mocks religion, the family, and "traditional values," and that makes explicit or suggestive sexual appeals.

It has not been uncommon for evangelical Christians to give up trying to come to terms with "secular" popular culture, and to boycott it altogether. But often they have simultaneously endorsed the creation of an extensive parallel popular culture, complete with Christian rock bands and night clubs, Christian soap operas and talk shows, Christian spy and romance novels, and Christian exercise videos. They have thus succeeded in being of the world, but not in the world.

This "Christian" popular culture takes all its cues from its secular counterpart, but sanitizes and customizes it with "Jesus language." In its crassest forms, it has simply substituted "Christian" language and imagery for elements in the original version: stealing the Coca-Cola theme, "It's the real thing," and using it to market Jesus ("He's the Real Thing"), for example. One of the earlier instances of this, in the late 1960s, was the rather tame folk-pop musical by Kurt Kaiser and Ralph Carmichael (the Henri Mancini of Christian music), "Natural High," which not only borrowed musical idioms from popular music, but borrowed the much more sinister physiological metaphor of drug-induced euphoria as well. It was brilliant marketing, right? Jesus is kind of like drugs, without the paraphernalia or sleazy pushers. *That* should appeal to our troubled youth.

STRIVING TO CONFORM TO THE WORLD

The extent to which the principle of "of the world, but not in the world" operates is illustrated by a "Music Comparison Chart" in the book *Contemporary Christian Music,* by Paul Baker.[1] In addition to columns that classify the musical style of the artists in question (Techno-pop, Rockabilly/Nostalgic Rock, Reggae, etc.), Baker includes a column headed "Sounds Like . . ." So we learn, for example, that Scott Wesley Brown sounds like Barry Manilow, or T-Bone Burnett sounds like Bob Dylan, John Lennon, and/or Roger McGuinn. Jamie Owens-Collins sounds like Olivia Newton-John and/or Juice Newton (but not, we assume, like Wayne Newton). Noel Paul Stookey sounds like (surprise) Peter, Paul and Mary. "The main thing to remember in using the chart is what it suggests," explains Baker. "If you like (or liked) artist 'A' in secular music, then there's a good chance you'll like some of the music of 'B' in Christian music." A small percentage of artists on Baker's chart are marked with an asterisk, which means that "an artist has developed his or her own recognizable sound, often with no direct parallel among the better known secular artists."

Now there's nothing unusual about entertainers who are reminiscent of other, and better, performers. James Coburn reminds a lot of people of a budget version of Lee Marvin, Julian Lennon sounds like his father, the work of film composer John Williams sounds like Gustav Holst or Ralph Vaughn Williams or Richard Strauss or whoever. What is disturbing is that Christian performers seem at times to achieve popularity because they sound like "secular" originals who are not quite kosher because they write dirty lyrics or bite the heads off of rodents or exhibit severe gender confusion in their wardrobes. It's disturbing because it seems as if the "good guys" are working very hard to measure up to the standards already set by the "bad guys." And the reason they professionally *need* to do this is because their potential audience demands it. After all, they're listening to the radio like the rest of their friends, and they *really* do like certain performers, but they know their parents would just *really* die if they ever figured out what the lyrics were, so like there's this Christian guy who sounds just like George Michael, only he doesn't say I want your sex, it's I want your soul, and it's really Jesus talking, but it sounds just like George Michael, right? And maybe we can sing it in church.

SELLING SOAP AND JESUS

Overstated? I don't think so. But is it really *wrong*? After all, there is nothing new about stealing useful cultural forms and artifacts to serve the interests of the gospel. John lifted the idea for his *Logos* Christology from contemporary philosophy, Paul quoted pagan poets, and Luther borrowed tunes from drinking songs for hymns. A vocalist named Dave Boyer established popularity a decade or two ago because he reminded his fans of Frank Sinatra or Jack Jones or another fifties-style crooner. If we were in a seminary class on missions, we might call this "sounds like" phenomonon an example of contextualization.

But the key word in this business is *useful*. How useful is it to borrow a cultural form if that form effectively cancels out the content you're using it to communicate? There are many instances of some very dubious borrowings in the history of the Church. As missionaries have taken the gospel to new cultures, it has always been tempting to recast the message of redemption in familiar forms. But some of those forms have been inappropriate as vehicles of holy truth, either because they introduced fatal distortion or misunderstanding, or because they were so intertwined with ungodly practices that their affiliation with the gospel seemed to sanction the very behavior the gospel should have challenged.

More subtly, achieving popularity by "sounding like" establishes a curious pattern for people striving to avoid being conformed to the pattern of this world. The implicit message of such celebrity is that Christians are successful to the extent that they mimic the models established by the world.

Early in the 1980s, the Christian Broadcasting Network (CBN) experimented with a Christian soap opera. CBN hired directors, writers, and actors who had experience in the secular soaps. The scripts had a typical soapy feel to them, the sets and camera angles were stock daytime fare, the music had the same melodramatic feel to it. What was different was the fact that a few of the characters were Christians, who occasionally spoke of the role their faith played in meeting soap-opera crises.

Shortly after the show began production, I spoke with a number of the people involved with the program, asking whether the conventions of soap operas didn't pose some challenges to presenting a Christian message. After all, it was a television genre that depended on the dramatic equivalent of gossip. None of the actors or production staff had given the possible conflict between form and content a minute's thought. One senior figure on the show said it didn't matter if you were selling soap or Jesus; hey, it's called "show business," right? It's all just a matter of using the right techniques to get people to "buy" the product. If you liked secular soap opera villain "A," you'll love our Christian soap opera villain "B," because she gets saved sometime next season. But meanwhile she's just as nasty as her "secular" counterpart.

What's wrong with this picture? Obviously (or maybe not so obviously; none of the people I talked to experienced what the psychologists call cognitive dissonance) the "of the world, but not in the world" strategy is not an adequate way of dealing with popular culture. The thin Christian veneer in such projects very quickly wears away, and what is *underneath* determines the response of consumers of such products. Such a strategy is a sad reminder that most of the Christian criticism of popular culture has focused on *content* while ignoring *form*. A generation after

Marshall McLuhan, the Church still behaves as if the forms of culture, especially the forms of mass media and the role they play in our lives, are value-neutral.

A FAITH FOR THE COMMON MAN

Despite the perennial protests over sex and violence on television, lewd rock lyrics, and pornography sold at convenience stores, evangelical Christians remain relatively oblivious to the problems associated with popular culture. This is in part because American evangelicalism has its roots in *populist* culture. Nathan O. Hatch has observed that "the genius of evangelicals long has been their firm identification with people. While others may have excelled in defending and elaborating the truth, and in building institutions to weather the storms of time, evangelicals in America have been passionate about communicating a message."[2] Evangelicals have always been partial to (in fact, they may even be defined by their sympathy to) great communicators, from John Wesley and George Whitefield, to Charles G. Finney, Dwight L. Moody, and Billy Sunday, to the greatest communicator of the twentieth century: television.

Popular culture is attractive to many conservative Christians precisely because it is . . . well, popular. It is the *people's* culture, and the people are whom evangelicals evangelize. With the overarching demand of the Great Commission looming over every evangelical enterprise, it is very easy to go for ratings instead of rationality, quantity rather than quality. Evangelicals have always been anti-elitist. Not for them the distant authority of a Magisterium or the speculative aridity of academic theologians. Give them instead a rousing pulpiteer. As Hatch observes, evangelicals tend to measure "the importance of an issue by its popular reception. By this logic, any position worth its salt will command a significant following. A best seller by definition becomes a 'classic'; to be read is to deserve to be read."[3]

The problems with such an attitude were anticipated by Alexis de Tocqueville, who warned of a "tyranny of the majority" in the young democracy, in which truth, goodness, and beauty would be determined by vote. A society that cultivates commonness, that is suspicious of genius, that has more esteem for the entrepreneur who caters to the tastes of the many than the visionary who challenges the spirits of the few — such a society is always in danger of defining worth in terms of immediate demand rather than eternal significance.

But we are getting ahead of ourselves. We have not heard enough evidence to call for the jury's verdict. Many readers may think I have rushed to judge popular culture too quickly and too harshly. But most would agree that popular culture has *some* intrinsic problems associated with it. If this is so, such problems will be evident whether they are part of the parallel Christian culture or the original secular version. It could even be that the sanitized clone is even *more* problematic, since *it* is assumed to be safe. (After all, "Christian" popular culture influences thousands of church services every Sunday morning. How could anything be wrong with it?) But any criticism of popular culture cannot afford to criticize only the *secular* variety. Since the forms and the way they are used are virtually identical, any valuable analysis will apply equally well to Johnny Carson and to Pat Robertson, to Linda Ronstadt and to Amy Grant.

Since "Christian" pop culture is something of a parasite on earlier forms, our principal attention will be given to the host. This will require that we understand the roots and the history of popular culture, its relationship to what are sometimes called "high culture" and "folk culture," and its entwining with a number of social and historical phenomena. It will also require that we understand the Biblical and theological criteria for obedient cultural life before God. Popular culture is not a simple, homogenous abstraction that allows for simple application of Biblical principles. Its challenges and temptations do not confront us like the proverbial harlot whose seductions are clearly to sin, straightforward and simple. It has many dimensions and contours and hidden agendas that require some historical and experiential perspective before we can evaluate it fairly and, having understood it, conduct ourselves in its presence with wisdom.

WHAT IS CULTURE, THAT THOU ART MINDFUL OF IT?

FIDDLING ON THE BRINK OF HELL

In a sermon given in 1939 at Oxford, C. S. Lewis raised the question: What are all of us doing here studying philosophy or medieval literature, while Europe is at war? "Why should we — indeed how can we — continue to take an interest in these placid occupations when the lives and liberties of our friends and the liberties of Europe are in the balance? Is it not like fiddling while Rome burns?"[1]

Lewis went on to argue that the Christian faces precisely that question even during peacetime. "To a Christian," he observed, "the true tragedy of Nero must be not that he fiddled while the city was on fire but that he fiddled on the brink of hell."[2]

Lewis then posed the question of the worth of Christians taking an interest in culture, particularly the academic study of culture. "Every Christian who comes to a university must at all times face a question compared with which the questions raised by war are relatively unimportant. He must ask himself how it is right, or even psychologically possible, for creatures who are every moment advancing either to heaven or hell, to spend any fraction of the little time allowed them in this world on such comparative trivialities as literature or art, mathematics or biology."[3]

Lewis's reply was that the ideal of suspending all cultural activity for the sake of evangelism or the pursuit of holiness was impossible. "If you attempted," he argued, "to suspend your whole intellectual and aesthetic activity, you would only succeed in substituting a worse cultural life for a better." This is precisely what many religious people do, which is one of the reasons we have such bad music and ugly architecture in Christian settings. Lewis went on:

> You are not, in fact, going to read nothing, either in the Church or on the [front] line: if you don't read good books you will read bad ones. If you don't go on thinking rationally, you will think irrationally. If you reject aesthetic satisfactions you will fall into sensual satisfactions.[4]

We cannot afford to be indifferent about culture any more than we can afford to be indifferent about the toxicity of the water we drink or the air we breathe. Even if we believe that the church is a kind of eschatological parenthesis in the history of redemption, we are still faced with real choices about how we spend our time and resources so as best to love God with all our being and love our neighbor.

The experience of popular culture is a bit different from that of high culture. Studying the works of J. S. Bach or John Donne systematically will likely afford us a better appreciation of them. But few people argue that a careful, rigorous, painstaking analysis of the compositions of Oingo Boingo will result in an enhanced perception of their records.

Most study of popular culture is concerned with sociological or political rather than aesthetic questions. Read any issue of the *Journal of Popular Culture*, and you are likely to see articles on topics such as animal rights and the circus geek, or a title such as "Class and Gender in Traveling Salesman Jokes: A Dialectical Deconstruction." If Lewis's colleagues were raising these sorts of questions, he probably would have enjoined them to get out to the front.

One reason aesthetic questions rarely arise in the study of popular culture is that cultural relativism is so well-entrenched;

it is generally assumed that questions of *taste* merely reflect *political* interests rather than any transcendent order of beauty or propriety. A Christian assessment of popular culture must take social *and* aesthetic perspectives in view. Culture is not (as many scholars today believe) simply the battleground for a perpetual war of classes, races, and genders. Such battles do occur, but they have much less to do with determining the quality of life in a culture than ideological academics imagine.

Culture has very much to do with the human spirit. What we find beautiful or entertaining or moving is rooted in our *spiritual* life. Most modern social critics are concerned about culture in general and popular culture in particular because of the political and economic consequences of certain cultural arrangements. They are obsessed with questions of power. But there is a realm of human experience that is prior to power. It is the imagination, and it has profound significance in shaping human history and in assisting (or opposing) moral and spiritual ends. The aesthetic aspects of culture are much closer to the spiritual core of experience than are sociological considerations. T. S. Eliot has noted that aesthetic sensibility and spiritual perception are very closely related. But of course, there are *social* forces that encourage or discourage certain aesthetic choices, and our study will not ignore them.

CULTURE AND RELIGION

Any adequate definition of culture seems so encompassing as to include everything in human experience. One nineteenth-century anthropologist offered this definition: "Culture is that complex whole which includes knowledge, belief, art, morals, law, custom, and any other capabilities and habits acquired by man as a member of society." One would like to have asked this scholar exactly what culture *excludes*.

Defining culture, as it turns out, is not at all an easy task. We can easily come up with a dictionary definition, and it would look something like the one in the previous paragraph. But such a definition, while helpful, is a bit like the classic definition of man as a featherless biped. It tells us how to recognize the thing defined, but it doesn't tell us much about how it behaves.

Jolly Hermann Göring, World War I flying ace and head of Hitler's *Luftwaffe*, is alleged to have offered a more practical perspective on culture. "When I hear anyone talk of culture," he warned, "I reach for my revolver."

In 1948, T. S. Eliot wrote an essay over a hundred pages long called "Notes Towards the Definition of Culture."[5] Eliot took a more normative than descriptive approach to defining culture. He wrote that culture may be described "simply as that which makes life worth living. And it is what justifies other peoples and other generations in saying, when they contemplate the remains and the influence of an extinct civilisation, that it was worth while for that civilisation to have existed."[6]

In the course of making his "Notes," Eliot saw that there are great affinities between culture and religion. No culture, argued Eliot, "can appear or develop except in relation to a religion."[7] Eliot believed that the same religion may inform a variety of cultures, but he questioned whether any culture could come into being without some sort of religious basis. Religion and culture, Eliot argued, are in a sense two aspects of the same thing. This means that culture cannot be preserved or developed without religion, an argument that many Christians have been presenting to twentieth-century secularists. But Eliot insisted that it *also* means that religion cannot be preserved or maintained without the preservation and maintenance of culture.

We must be careful to be modest in appropriating Eliot's insights, because in the next paragraph of his essay Eliot said that this way of looking at religion and culture "is so difficult that I am not sure I grasp it myself except in flashes, or that I comprehend all its implications." If *he* didn't quite understand what he was saying, we don't want to be too quick to assume that *we* do. But a more serious problem with accepting Eliot's prescriptions too easily is that he was assuming a society in which there is an established church. In his earlier essay, "The Idea of a Christian Society" (1940), he clearly said that "such a society can only be realised when the great majority of the sheep belong to the same fold."[8] He meant the same *institutional* church. Eliot believed that the separation of church and state on the American model, while it avoided many problems, created problems of its own, among them the virtual impossibility of a Christian society or a Christian culture as he understood it.

CULTURE AND RELATIVISM

But for our present purposes, Eliot at least serves to focus attention on the relationship between culture and some transcendent norms. In the study of culture, argued Eliot, "the most important question that we can ask, is whether there is any permanent standard, by which we can compare one civilisation with another."[9] If there *are* transcendent norms for assessing culture, a number of things happen. First of all, we are forced to fight *cultural relativism*, that nasty habit all too common in the twentieth century to assume that all values that have some tie with one's culture are simply created by that culture, that all cultures create different values, and that it is simply egocentric and chauvinistic to prefer one set of values to another. Allan Bloom's *The Closing of the American Mind*[10] should have marked the death of cultural relativism. As Bloom argued, "the fact that there have been different opinions about good and bad in different times and places in no way proves that none is superior to others. . . . On the face of it, the difference of opinion would seem to raise the question as to which is true or right rather than to banish it. The natural reaction is to try to resolve the difference, to examine the claims and reasons for each opinion."[11]

Cultural relativism is one of the dominant assumptions of modern American culture. In addition to being a great obstacle to clear thinking about culture, it is one of the great enemies of Christianity, since all good cultural relativists would have to say that Christianity as we understand it is just a product of Western culture. The idea that the Bible makes universal truth-claims is absurd, since there's no such thing.

Cultural relativism not only makes it impossible to assert that, for example, Thomas Jefferson is a more significant thinker than a headhunter from Borneo; it also makes it impossible to claim that Thomas Jefferson is a more significant thinker than Bruce Springsteen. Cultural relativism cuts in several planes. It denies the possibility that one society's culture might be superior to another's, and it denies the possibility that one form of cultural expression might be superior to another form *within the same culture*.

Eliot says that if, on the other hand, there are permanent standards by which we can measure a culture, or some aspect of it, "we can distinguish between higher and lower cultures; we can distinguish between advance and retrogression."[12] Not only can we say that some cultures are in certain ways superior to others, and that some cultural phenomena are superior to others within the same culture, we can also look at whether a culture is in a period of cultural progress or cultural decline.

As Christians, we insist that there *are* permanent standards for culture. Culture is the human effort to give structure to life. But human nature does not exist as a law unto itself. Human nature is, as part of God's creation, a permanent standard. Men and women cannot act against their own nature without violating the standards God has established in their very being. Moreover, the rest of creation, in which culture is established and with which culture must always contend, has a divinely established order. Cultural institutions, artifacts, and expressions that deny, suppress, or distort that order ought to be recognized as inferior to those that acknowledge, honor, and enjoy it.

CULTURE IN CONTEXT

Culture is an abstraction. We cannot isolate for observation three pounds or fourteen centimeters of culture. These abstract questions of definition are extremely important, just as some amount of abstract thinking about who God is and what man is are necessary if we want to be obedient to God. But responsible evaluation of culture must always deal with concrete human experience of what has been labeled "culture." We don't, after all, encounter *culture*. We hear a particular song or see a specific film or read a novel that we have chosen from among all the others available.

Not only does cultural analysis require that we look at real cultural experiences, it requires that we look at them in their natural habitat, and that we understand something of their history.

In assessing rock 'n' roll, for example, it's not enough to read the lyrics and find out on what beat of each measure the accent falls. We also need to consider what relationship rock has with other aspects of pop culture, what social role it plays for its fans, and how it compares with other musical options available to listeners. We need to look at the *culture* of rock, not just the words and the music.

Such consideration of the context of a particular cultural expression is important not for the sake of some sort of academic purity, but for the sake of Christian wisdom. Many of the decisions we make about our involvement in popular culture are not really questions about good and evil. When I decide not to read a certain book, I am not necessarily saying that to read it would be a sin. It is much more likely that I believe it to be imprudent to take the time to read that book at this time in my life. To paraphrase Paul's argument in 1 Corinthians 10 (which is, as we shall see, a very significant passage for our thinking about culture), something may be permissible, but it may not be very beneficial or constructive.

Each of us arises every morning with, in the providence of God, a number of duties, dilemmas, opportunities, and confusions that stem from living in a particular culture at a particular time. Our decisions about what sort of involvement with popular culture is prudent does not occur in isolation. Just as a critic cannot understand a song or a novel or a movie outside of its cultural context, so we cannot anticipate or evaluate the effect popular culture has on our lives without looking at that context. Do I want to read that book because everyone else is reading it, or because of some intrinsic merit it has? Am I turning on the television because there is something I want to watch, or because I am addicted to distracting titillation?

CULTURE AND SOCIAL ENGINEERING

No particular form of popular culture is inevitable. It is not ultimately the product of a conspiracy of media magnates or secular humanist gurus. The more we study culture in its total context, the more we are impressed with the fact that it is the result of billions of separate choices by millions of people. As T. S. Eliot observed, culture "is the product of a variety of more or less harmonious activities, each pursued for its own sake: the artist must concentrate upon his canvas, the poet upon his typewriter, the civil servant upon the just settlement of particular problems as they present themselves upon his desk, each according to the situation in which he finds himself."[13]

Rarely if ever is the condition of a culture the product of deliberate decision, either by the society as a whole or by a group of social engineers, whether elected or self-appointed. Cultural development is something that occurs naturally rather than artificially. It is never contrived. To be sure, particular artifacts in popular culture (as well as in high culture) are the product of deliberate activity, but rarely is that activity intended to produce some huge, cultural effect. When the television was invented, it wasn't because some malevolent engineers wanted to open a Pandora's box for society. When Norman Lear decided to produce *All in the Family*, it was certainly a departure from television programming that had gone before, but no one could have predicted that the show would be accepted by the audience, and would in turn influence the standards of the audience. The viewers decided that for themselves. Perhaps the critics helped, but nobody has to listen to critics.

Those who condemn attempts at social engineering are correct in noting that all efforts to remake society (let alone human nature) are destined to fail because no would-be reformer of society has enough knowledge about all of the interrelationships of that complex reality called "society" to anticipate how tinkering with some of the parts will affect other parts and the whole. The belief that "planners" can predict what their efforts at reform will produce is what Friedrich Hayek calls the "fatal conceit."

The same call to humility should be given to those of us who want to effect a change in culture. Cultural engineering doesn't work. We can do very little to encourage or discourage cultural trends or fads. We can do something, however. As Eliot noted, "we can combat the intellectual errors and the emotional prejudices which stand in the way" of cultural change.[14] That is, we can call attention to the folly or absurdity or outright sin that certain cultural phenomena encourage or facilitate. Eliot's call to cultural humility is sobering, and is consistent not only with a realistic view of human culture, but with a Biblical view of the pervasiveness of human sin.

> We should look for the improvement of society, as we seek our own individual improvement, in relatively minute particulars. We cannot say: "I shall make myself into a different person"; we can only say: "I will give up this bad habit, and endeavour to contract this good one." So of society we can only say: "We shall try to improve it in this respect or the other, where excess or defect is evident: we must try at the same time to embrace so much in our view, that we may avoid, in putting one thing right, putting something else wrong." Even this is to express an aspiration greater than we can achieve: for it is as much, or more, because of what we do piecemeal without understanding or foreseeing the consequences, that the culture of one age differs from that of its predecessor.[15]

CULTURE AND BIBLICAL NORMS

In the next chapter, we will be looking at Biblical teaching about culture in general and about the general obligations of individual believers within an unbelieving culture. As we do that, we need to keep in mind what culture *is*. Applying Scripture to our individual experience is difficult for each of us, often as much because we fail to understand the significance of our own situation, the context in which we are applying it, as because we fail to understand the original, objective meaning of the text. We live in complex patterns of need, of opportunity, and of sin, and the inference we really ought to draw from Scripture is often the most difficult to see, because of the complexity and sin in our lives. This is why we need teachers and the fellowship of the saints.

The first thing we must do, and I'm afraid it is done all too little, is to come up with some principles for interpreting and applying the Scriptures to this huge abstraction called *culture*.

What sort of being *is* a culture? It's not a person. It's not even an institution, like the church or the state or the family. It is instead a dynamic pattern, an ever-changing matrix of objects, artifacts, sounds, institutions, philosophies, fashions, enthusiasms, myths, prejudices, relationships, attitudes, tastes, rituals, habits, colors, and loves, all embodied in individual people, in groups and collectives and associations of people (many of whom do not know they are associated), in books, in buildings, in the use of time and space, in wars, in jokes, and in food.

We can't simplify things too quickly by isolating one of these cultural expressions and asking how Scripture applies to *it* in isolation from everything else, for then it's not part of that social experience that's called culture. We cannot, for example, evaluate the virtues and vices of fast food in our culture merely by looking at Biblical teaching about meals. We have to take into consideration the place of the automobile and highways in our culture, our view of time and convenience, the pressures on modern families (both those relieved and those exacerbated by fast food), the opportunity for employment created by this new service industry, and many other pieces of the cultural puzzle. We then have to ask, given all of the other forces that shape modern culture, whether eliminating McDonald's from the equation would mean that people would automatically eat more nutritious home-cooked meals with the family gathered around the table, or whether they would eat more frozen TV dinners on their own unsynchronized schedules.

Having defined a specific cultural thing about which we are trying to draw inferences from Scripture, we can then try to place it in the context of what Scripture says about culture and the place of the Christian within a culture shared with unbelievers.

All the while, we need to keep in mind the Biblical call to wisdom. Living in a culture that is increasingly hostile to Christian living is one of the more consistent trials we will face. James quite clearly tells us that trials require wisdom, and if any of us lacks wisdom, we should ask God, and He will give it (1:5). The Biblical call to get wisdom is a thread that runs through much of Scripture. In commenting on the so-called "Wisdom Literature" in the Bible (i.e., Proverbs, Job, and Ecclesiastes),

Derek Kidner notes that the tone of voice is very distinct from that in the Law and the Prophets.

> The blunt "Thou shalt" or "shalt not" of the Law, and the urgent "Thus saith the Lord" of the Prophets, are joined now by the cooler comments of the teacher and the often anguished questions of the learner. Where the bulk of the Old Testament calls us simply to obey and believe, this part of it . . . summons us to think hard as well as humbly; to keep our eyes open, to use our conscience and our common sense, and not to shirk the most disturbing questions.[16]

Saying that wisdom calls us to think is hardly a denial of God's authority, or to suggest that God is indifferent about what decisions we make. Pascal once said that the first of all moral obligations is to think clearly, and the Proverbs are quite emphatic that obedience to God requires "a disciplined and prudent life" (Proverbs 1:3), which must surely involve clear thinking.

Derek Kidner points out how the call to reflection that is represented by the Wisdom Literature is a recognition and reminder that God's Law is imprinted in the very structure of creation.

> This demand for thought presupposes a world that answers to thought. Not, to be sure, one which we can hope to master with our finite minds; but that is our limitation, not the world's; for if it is a creation, and the product of perfect wisdom, it will be in principle intelligible. So even when the arrogance of human thought has to be rebuked . . . the Old Testament makes no retreat into notions of divine caprice; still less, of "a tale told by an idiot" or nobody at all. Instead, it sees God's wisdom expressed and echoed everywhere — except where man, the rebel, has presumed to disagree and to disrupt the pattern.[17]

As we shall see in the following chapter, culture is regarded by Scripture as an extension of creation. It is, after all, fabricated by created (if fallen) human nature and created (if fallen) human will, interacting with the necessities of living in the created (if fallen) world. The demand of Scripture to pursue wisdom by reflecting on revelation in creation (as well as in the Word) requires that we spend some time pondering human culture. We should "consider" the jaded television producer and the screaming fans of Michael Jackson, even as we consider the ant and the lilies of the field.

WOULD YOU TAKE JESUS TO SEE THIS PLANET?

AFTER THE SEVENTH DAY, BEFORE THE LAST DAY

Should the culture of Christians be separate from the culture of the unbelieving world? Should Christians isolate themselves from the culture around them, or should they be trying to take it over, or something in between? Is the culture we now share with unbelievers only a source of temptation and grief, or can it somehow be "redeemed"?

These are some of the fundamental questions we have to ask of Scripture. One thing that is clear at the outset is that, at this time in history, in God's providential ordering of things, the covenant community of the people of God is scattered, dispersed within broader human cultures. Some of these cultures have been shaped to a significant degree by the Church; others have no Christian influence whatsoever. It was not always so. After the giving of the Law and before the coming of Christ, the people of God had a totally parochial and segregated culture. Israel was called to be holy and was given special instructions about how to exhibit that holiness in its culture, because their God was holy and they were a special people before God. Israel's holy culture was a visible but partial recovery of the original holy culture in the Garden of Eden, and a foretaste of the holy culture God's people will enjoy in eternity. The distinctiveness of the people of

Israel was a sign of obedience to God, a sign evident to them-selves and to the world. It was a distinctiveness that extended to the kind of food they could eat and how it was to be prepared, the kind of clothing they could wear, and where they should dig their latrines.

In trying to understand Biblical teaching about culture, we can't just look at one phase of the history of God's redemptive work. The Bible tells a single story of redemption, but it has many chapters. It begins with creation and ends with a vision of a new heaven and a new earth. In between are the formative experiences and expectations of the patriarchs; the holy but often disobedient nation of Israel (living at times in liberty and at times in captivity); the earthly sojourn of Jesus, the God-Man, to bear judgment and to defeat sin and death; and the Spirit-led exuber-ance of the early Church. We live "between the times," in the "already but not yet" tension between the accomplishment of redemption and the final judgment. Figuring out what to make of culture will involve determining how the experience of God's people in this distinctive time of redemptive history resembles and differs from that of other periods.

AND IT WAS SO

Much theological thinking about culture properly begins with creation, since human culture was part of man's life as he was created. Theologians speak of Genesis 1:28 as the "creation mandate." Hidden in the seed of this text is the great flowering of all human culture: God blessed man, male and female, created in His image, and said: "Be fruitful and increase in number; fill the earth and subdue it. Rule over the fish of the sea and the birds of the air and over every living creature that moves on the ground."

In the parallel narrative of creation in Genesis 2, we see God placing Adam in the Garden of Eden "to work it and take care of it" (2:15). God also brought all the animals "to the man to see what he would name them; and whatever the man called each living creature, that was its name" (2:19ff.).

Man's earliest cultural activity involved the ordering of creation. God created the Garden as something that needed care, and man as someone that had agricultural skills. In the naming of the animals, we witness the earliest form of man's innate ability to use language to describe creation and to organize it in some systematic fashion. The name each animal was given was the name it kept; Adam didn't give a new name to each animal every day. Those names were something that made it possible for him to talk about the animals; Adam would later tell his wife and his children those names. They became part of their culture. Perhaps they sang songs and wrote verse that used those earliest animal names. The abstraction of a name for each animal even made it possible for Adam to think about the animals more fully.

Culture, as we see it originate in Genesis, was intended by God to be a fulfillment of the image of God, an imitation of God. Man was called to be a worker, like the Divine Worker who established the model in the six days of creation. Old Testament scholar Meredith Kline observes: "Fulfillment of man's cultural stewardship would thus begin with man functioning as princely gardener in Eden." Kline goes on to argue that Genesis 1:28 indicates that, in placing man in Eden, God was not limiting man's cultural goals to some "minimal, local life support system." Rather, "the cultural mandate put all the capacity of human brain and brawn to work in a challenging and rewarding world to develop his original paradise home into a universal city."[1]

It is difficult to imagine what Adam and Eve thought of the command by their Creator to subdue the whole earth. Most of us have trouble keeping our lawns mowed and our gutters clean. Of course, we live in a fallen world. Nonetheless, it must have been an exuberating challenge to consider exercising obedient dominion over an entire planet.

This cultural mandate was by nature a religious duty. As Kline observes: "Invited to be a fellow laborer with God — that is the dignity of man the worker and the zest and glory of man's labor. Jesus, the second Adam, affirmed his own adherence to the imitation of God principle in this particular respect when he said: 'My Father works until now and I work' (John 5:17)."[2]

Kline continues:

God's work was creative, sustaining, governing; so too, on a creaturely level, was man's. God's original works of absolute origination found analogues in man's constructive and inventive activities, in his artistic creativity, and in his procreative functioning. . . . In man's cultivation of the earth, his nourishing and nurturing of his own young, his caring for and using, taming and domesticating the animals, in all the variety of his cultural laboring to subdue the earth, he was imitating what God did in his providential preserving and governing of the world as a place which through its fulness of provision supported man's bodily life and through its harmonies and its infinities answered to the deep call of the human spirit.[3]

Man was fit for the cultural mandate. As the bearer of his Creator-God's image, he could not be satisfied apart from cultural activity. Here is the origin of human culture in untainted glory and possibility. It is no wonder that those who see God's redemption as a transformation of human culture speak of it in terms of re-creation.

A WELL-DESERVED REST

But the most profound aspect of the creation culture was man's imitation of God in the Sabbath-rest. God the worker became God the rester on the seventh day. Genesis 2:2 describes God observing a rest on the seventh day. But Genesis 2:3 goes on with the further point that God also blessed the seventh day and sanctified it — that is, he made it a holy day, a day set apart.

It is important that we realize that the Sabbath was not something introduced by the giving of the Law on Mount Sinai; it was merely reiterated there. It is clear from Exodus 31 and other passages that the Sabbath was not some arbitrary ritual suggested by God for Israel's sake. Rather, it was established as holy in the very order of creation. Look at Exodus 31:12-18, the climax of Moses's forty days on Mount Sinai:

Then the Lord said to Moses, "Say to the Israelites, 'You must observe my Sabbaths. This will be a sign between me and you for the generations to come, so you may know that I am the Lord, who makes you holy.

"'Observe the Sabbath, because it is holy to you. Anyone who desecrates it must be put to death; whoever does any work on that day must be cut off from his people. For six days work is to be done, but the seventh day is a Sabbath of rest, holy to the Lord. Whoever does any work on the Sabbath day must be put to death. The Israelites are to observe the Sabbath, celebrating it for the generations to come as a lasting covenant. It will be a sign between me and the Israelites forever, for in six days the Lord made the heavens and the earth, and on the seventh day he abstained from work and rested.'"

The Sabbath was a holy sign of the covenant bond between God and His people. It was as much a part of the order of creation as was creative labor, and in being obedient in work and rest, Israel would demonstrate its total allegience to God.

As the Sabbath (like work and marriage) is rooted in the nature of creation, it is certain that the Sabbath (like work and marriage) was part of the cultural experience of Eden. While we have no explicit mention of human observance of the Sabbath in the first chapters of Genesis, the arguments made in passages such as Exodus 31 about the nature of the Sabbath indicate that God's sanctifying of it (Genesis 2:2ff.) was from then on part of how creation functioned. The intimate fellowship between God and man in the Garden presupposes that man would honor what God had established as holy. Since the Fall is the first occurrence of human disobedience to the divine order established in creation, it is impossible that man would *not* have observed the Sabbath in the original culture of Eden.

In imitating God's rest in the Sabbath, man was called to demonstrate with religious regularity the divine source of his creativity and energy. As Kline puts it,

For man to observe the Sabbath in obedient imitation of the paradigm of work and rest established by his Creator was an acknowledgement that he was the Creator's servant-son, a confession of God as his Father and Lord. As an ordinance observed by man the Sabbath was a . . . confessional sign of man's consecration to God.

In observing the Sabbath, man was culturally structuring time in accordance with a holy pattern. This was part of his cultural commission, along with the task of being an architect in space by tending the Garden. Space and time were thus consecrated by man's original culture.

For man as originally created, there was no separation between his culture and his loving worship of his Lord. Culture and religious duty were one. All cultural activity was self-consciously pursued as an act of loving obedience. Not only the internal attitude of man in these activities, but the invention of the very cultural structures themselves, the external institutions of things, were bound to be a deliberate act of service to the Creator. Just as God's will and creative word called real planets and trees and birds and fish into being, so man's will, intellect, and imagination would effect the establishment of real art and science and agriculture and social structures. This was the sort of holism and unity many of us long for: no shadow between culture and devotion.

But then the Fall occurred.

AFTER EDEN

If we know anything about the story of Adam and Eve, we know that the result of the Fall, of rebellion against God, was the curse. God had warned Adam and Eve that they would die if they disobeyed. But their death was postponed, and a temporal curse, common to all mankind, was uttered by God. Ultimate judgment was delayed.

Genesis 3:14-19 contains the sobering words of the curse:

So the Lord God said to the serpent, "Because you have done this, Cursed are you above all the livestock and all the wild animals! You will crawl on your belly and you will eat dust all the days of your life. And I will put enmity between you and the woman, and between your offspring and hers; he will crush your head, and you will strike his heel."

To the woman he said, "I will greatly increase your pains in childbearing; with pain you will give birth to children. Your desire will be for your husband, and he will rule over you."

To Adam he said, "Because you listened to your wife and ate from the tree about which I commanded you, 'You must not eat of it,' Cursed is the ground because of you; through painful toil you will eat of it all the days of your life. It will produce thorns and thistles for you, and you will eat the plants of the field. By the sweat of your brow you will eat your food until you return to the ground, since from it you were taken; for dust you are and to dust you will return."

A number of commentators have noted that there are signs of God's grace *even in this curse*. The great Biblical scholar Geerhardus Vos pointed out that in promising to put enmity between the seed of the Tempter and the seed of the woman, God the sovereign Judge was taking the sovereign inititive to save man from destruction.

Man in sinning had sided with the serpent and placed himself in opposition to God. Now the attitude towards the serpent becomes one of hostility; this must carry with it a corresponding change in man's attitude towards God. God being the mover in the warfare against Satan, man, joining in this, becomes plainly the ally of God.[4]

The curse not only contained the seeds of salvation; it also assumed that God's providence in creation would allow human culture to continue, even though man was now alienated from God, the model for his cultural activity. One could imagine other alternatives. Man in sin could have been chained to a rock, or consigned to life in a cave or on the dark side of the moon. There is no reason for Adam and Eve to have expected even being granted visiting rights to the planet God had given them as their domain. But rather than removing them from the arena of their cultural life, God offered some cultural assistance. He clothed them when they experienced shame from their nakedness, their divinely fashioned garb a sign of the covering of sin that would eventually restore fellowship between God and man.

As Meredith Kline has noted, after the Fall, though child-birth would be painful, there would still be children; the race would continue. While tilling the soil would be arduous, the earth would still yield fruit, along with weeds and thorns.

> The world order continued. The sun was not darkened, the heavens did not pass away, the earth was not consumed. Man was not totally abandoned to the power of sin and the devil; he was not cast into outer darkness. The positive benefits realized in a measure through this restraint on the effects of sin and the curse are not the eternal benefits of the holy, heavenly kingdom that come to the elect through God's saving grace in Christ, but they are blessings — temporal blessings that all men experience in common by virtue of their remaining part of the continuing world order.[5]

But while cultural life continues, the reality of the common curse must not be understated. As Kline describes it:

> By reason of the common curse the history of mankind would be turned into a history of death. The ground man was to subdue would subdue him. . . . A shadow would be cast by the inevitability of death over all man's earthly exis-tence, making all his labors seem like a clutching at the wind. . . . Under the common curse, humanity was to be troubled by social discord as well as by afflictions in the realm of nature. . . . In sum, the common curse would turn human experience on earth into a struggle for survival, a per-petual conflict, a vain history unto death.[6]

No longer was cultural life the blissful blend of work and worship. No longer was man's cultural existence consecrated as a living offering to the God he loved. As subsequent passages of Genesis make clear, many human cultural activities were pursued as acts of wanton disobedience to God. The construction of the Tower of Babel is a monument to man's use of culture to serve his idolatrous ends.

WE WILL NEVER PASS THIS WAY AGAIN

The most significant moment in the story of the Fall is the expulsion from the Garden. Even more horrible than the promise of painful childbirth and difficult farming, even of the inevitability of death itself, was the eviction of Adam and Eve from this place favored by the special presence of God. The Garden was the original sanctuary, a holy place, and, as Kline notes:

> In his zeal for the sanctity of his own holy Name, God had come to cleanse his temple and he made a thorough work of it. By their apostasy the priests of the temple had turned it into an abomination. . . . Driven from his native homeland, the holy and blessed land, into a world profane and cursed, man is in exile on the face of the earth. His historical existence is a wandering east of Eden. Until the restoration of all things, the earth has taken on the character of a wilderness, lying outside the holy land of promise. It is a realm under the shadow of death. In the hour that God drove man into exile it was indicated that any future return to God's dwelling place and the tree of life must involve a passage through the flaming sword of God's judgment, with which the new guardians of his sanctuary were armed.[7]

The restoration of holy human culture requires the refining fire of judgment. This is why Israel's cultural life was marked by such severe penalties for disobedience: the sword of the cherubim must guard the culture that claims the sanction of God Himself. The holy culture of the new heaven and the new earth, in which lamb and lion lie side by side, requires first that judgment cleanse the evil that the Fall introduced. The Fall and the curse introduced a principle of death and conflict to human culture, a principle that will not be eradicated from the earth until the cleansing judgment of God. Re-creation, the recovery of the creation experience of culture, the returning to the blessed environment of the Garden, can only take place when judgment is a present reality.

But judgment has been delayed. While many of Christ's disciples believed that He was coming to judge, it became clear that His first coming was to *bear* judgment, not to *exercise* it. His return in glory will be the occasion for inaugurating a holy culture once again.

CULTURE OF A KILLER

Meanwhile, culture cannot have the holy quality it had in the Garden, though culture continues to serve lesser needs of man. It is interesting to note that Scripture records an amazing amount of cultural activity in the line of Cain. Remember, the line of Cain was identified with the line of rebellion against God because of Cain's wicked act of fratricide. In Genesis 4:17 we read that Cain built a city. In verse 20 we are told of Jabal: "He was the father of those who live in tents and raise livestock." In the next verse we meet Jubal: "He was the father of all who play the harp and flute." Tubal-cain, introduced in verse 22, was the forger of "all kinds of tools out of bronze and iron."

Clearly, human culture of all sorts was thriving in this evil family. In chapter 5, describing the line of Seth, the faithful line that produced Enoch and Noah, we read of no significant cultural achievements. The only special feature in the line of Seth was Enoch (who "walked with God, and he was not, for God took him") and Methuselah, who lived to be 969. Methuselah's son was Lamech, and Lamech's son was Noah.

At the time of Noah, we read that God had become especially grieved at the wickedness of man. So God decided to wipe mankind from the face of the earth — all mankind, that is, except the family of Noah, who "found favor in the eyes of the Lord."

The story of the Flood and its immediate aftermath has a great deal to teach us about the nature of human culture. First of all, there are significant parallels between the covenant with Noah, developed in Genesis 8, 9, and 10, and the original ordinances of creation. In 9:1, God blessed Noah and told him and his sons to be fruitful and multiply and fill the earth. In verse 2, He talked of the dominion that man would have over all the beasts. This is all reminiscent of the vocation God gave Adam.

But there are some important discontinuities between the two episodes. In Genesis 9:3, there was a removal of the dietary restrictions that had been placed on Noah and his family while they were in the ark. In Genesis 7, when God was giving Noah instructions for gathering animals into the ark, He distinguished between clean and unclean animals, and told Noah to take more of the clean animals; they would be needed for sacrifices and for food.

So while they were in the ark, sovereignly protected by God from the waters of judgment, Noah and his family had to observe special dietary restrictions. Such restrictions seem to have significance in Scripture as emblems of holiness. Israel's diet was restricted because Israel's culture was holy. But that restriction would be revoked for Noah and his family when they emerged from the ark and began the task of restoring human culture.

But the covenant with Noah, sworn at the same time the dietary restrictions were lifted, was a restricted covenant. It covered temporal blessings. It was, in fact, a covenant made with creation: Genesis 9:9ff. tells us that God was making a covenant not only with Noah and his descendants, but with "the birds, the livestock and all the wild animals, all those that came out of the ark with you — every living creature on earth." The promise of that covenant was that God would never destroy the earth again by flood. In other words, the covenant with Noah was a covenant for all humanity and all creation, not for a special holy people.

The first thing Noah did after this covenant was established was to plant a vineyard. He was, after all, a "man of the soil." The next recorded action of Noah was to get drunk from the wine of his vineyard and pass out naked in his tent. This hardly seems the sort of action worthy of the father of all subsequent mankind. The next major event recorded after this episode was the attempt to raise the Tower of Babel. Human culture after the Flood and the rainbow did not seem to be getting off to a very good start.

If I seem a bit irreverent, it is because the text invites it. I think Noah's binge is included in the text in part to keep us from making the mistake of thinking that the fresh start for creation meant a return to the state of affairs before the Fall. Clearly, this was not the case. Noah and his family got off to a bad start, but we should have expected no more. The deliverance of Noah and his family from the destruction of the Flood was a victory for mankind as such, but it was not a decisive victory for the people of God.

The later deliverance of the people of God from the judgment-waters of the Red Sea was a very different matter. In that case, the beneficiaries of God's favor were delivered from bondage and from judgment in order to swear a holy covenant with their God. But meanwhile, outside of Israel, among the nations, human culture as such, the culture in the tradition of the line of Cain, continued.

THE COMMON CULTURE

In Noah's family after the Flood, we see God addressing man as man, both the elect and the nonelect. While there were rules given for human society (including a prohibition on murder and the institution of capital punishment), there were no obligations given to man as man to conform all human culture to a holy pattern.

When Israel's culture was established, it was both a partial recovery of the original experience in Eden and a typological anticipation of the final, fulfilled Kingdom of God, in which culture and worship would be one, in which there was no discontinuity between the human and the holy. But as we know from the sad story of Eden, the way back to that holy land is a way that involves judgment. As noted above, this is precisely why Israel's law was so rigorous. An Israelite could be stoned for breaking the Sabbath, for committing adultery, for being disrespectful to parents. Meanwhile, Israel pursued an unrelenting foreign policy of conquest and devastation: Take no prisoners; put all to the sword. This was very literally a holy war, a war that was a temporal manifestation — a life-size, bloody, audio-visual aid, if you will — that underscored the severity of God's judgment and the demands of His holiness. God's people were to be holy, for He was holy, and any violation of that holiness was to be met with banishment from the holy community, either by eviction or death.

Culture and holy congregation were one in Eden, they were one in Israel (though necessarily in an imperfect way), and they will be one again in the new heaven and the new earth. But since the typological life of Israel has passed, since its foreshadowing of God's final Kingdom in a real, flesh-and-blood geopolitical entity is not in God's plan between the two advents of Christ (in whom all the Law is fulfilled, and who will come with the final, devastating judgment at the Last Day), the Church must be content with being leaven within a common culture. It is not in the interest of the spreading of the gospel that God's people be a sequestered ethnic group any longer. The great message of the gospel is intended to go to the ends of the earth. To accomplish that, the people of God must be found in all cultures, eating and drinking, enjoying music and art and making tools with those who do not yet know the gospel.

This is the message of Acts 10. In that episode in the life of the early Church, Peter had a vision of a sheet being lowered, containing "all kinds of four-footed animals, as well as reptiles of the earth and birds of the air." Peter then heard a voice telling him that he could eat any of the animals. Peter refused three times (Peter seemed to do things in threes), saying that he had never eaten anything impure or unclean. In other words, as a good Jew he had worked hard to maintain the dietary restrictions of the holy culture established by God in the Law. Only later did he realize the meaning of the vision, when invited to the home of a Gentile. Arriving at the home of Cornelius, he said, "You are well aware that it is against our law for a Jew to associate with a Gentile or visit him. But God has shown me that I should not call any man impure or unclean."

Peter was among the first Christians to realize that the people of God in our epoch of redemptive history are not called to a segregated culture, but are called to take the gospel to all cultures. Israel's holy culture prevented Jews from associating or visiting with Gentiles. But the people of God in this new moment of redemptive history are not only *allowed* to visit with other peoples, they are *commanded* to do so. This is stated most dramatically by Paul who, in 1 Corinthians 10, says that believers shouldn't even worry about eating meat that had been sacrificed to idols, and should accept dinner invitations from unbelievers without worrying about what food was going to be served.

The culture of Israel was intended to demonstrate the holy eschatological reality of God's rule, but human culture *as such* cannot do that because human beings *as such* do not submit to the rule of God. Many Christians seem to miss that point. Nicholas Wolterstorff, in his book *Until Justice and Peace Embrace,* writes:

> If we had lived as God meant us to live, we would all be members of an ordered community bound together by love for each other and gratitude to God, using the earth for our benefit and delight. In fact we do not live thus. A fall has occurred. God's response to this fall of mankind was to choose from all humanity a people destined for eternal life.

Up to this point, Wolterstorff is right. He continues, "They in obedient gratitude are now to work for the renewal of human life so that it may become what God meant it to be." But exactly how can the Church "work for the renewal of human life"? That would seem to be something that God effects sovereignly. Our lives are renewed by him, and to the extent that we are obedient, what we do in the world will have a different quality to it. There are limits to what we can do for the simple reason that we're not the only ones here.

But let Wolterstorff finish. "They are to struggle to establish a holy commonwealth here on earth."[8] If by holy commonwealth he means the Church, that's fine. The Church is, after all, a holy nation and a royal priesthood. But the Church is a commonwealth only in a metaphoric sense. It doesn't have a representative at the U.N.; it doesn't maintain an army or put people in jail or issue driver's licenses or do any other things commonwealths do. Wolterstorff continues, "Of course it is [not was: is] the mandate of all humanity to struggle toward such a community." Well, no, it's not. There is *nothing* in the covenant with Noah, which is the most significant instance in Scripture of God addressing fallen mankind *en masse*, about *holiness*. There couldn't be.

It is most certainly *not* the mandate for all humanity to be struggling to build a holy community or commonwealth. Not even the *people of God* in our epoch of redemptive history are called to create a holy culture, because Christians are called to go out into every culture with the gospel. We are a people, to be sure, but our peoplehood is spiritual. Culturally, we are Jew and Gentile, Greek and Roman, European and African.

THE BODY OF CHRIST

But saying that human culture is not holy is not to say that it is worthless. It is still part of the image of God in us for men and women to pursue cultural activities. The experience of human culture in all its diversity is the way we enjoy being human. And enjoy it we must. Being human is the most profound aspect of the creation for which we ought to give thanks. If we can enjoy the beauty of all else in creation, how foolish to resent or ignore the image of the Creator, the pinnacle of creation. It is being human, not being saved — it is the image of God in us, not regeneration — that establishes the capacity to recognize the distinctions between the beautiful and the ugly, between order and chaos, between the creative and the stultifying.

We were created beings before we were redeemed beings. God's benediction on creation has not been entirely erased by the Fall. Jesus Himself is not only divine, He is human. Does He enjoy it, or simply endure it? Until our bodies are made new, like the body Jesus now enjoys, our calling is not to *escape* fleshly existence, nor to *sanctify* culture (since it is "common," shared by believer and unbeliever, and cannot be made holy), but to so influence our culture as to make it more consistent with the created nature of man, and to sanctify our own lives, because we are also living *in the Spirit*, with our minds set on the things that are above.

We acknowledge this distinction between the holy and the common each time we partake of the Lord's Supper. Every meal I eat, I eat to the glory of God, under the Lordship of Christ. But not every meal I eat has the significance and the power to transform that the Lord's Supper has. It is a holy meal in a way last week's visit to Burger King is not. Not everyone is allowed to eat this holy meal, but everyone *is* allowed to eat at Burger King. If there are deficiencies within the culture that have produced Burger King, the deficiencies are not due to the fact that it is not a holy place, but because it violates or compromises aspects of our experience as human beings. If we believe that to be the case, our goal as Christians would not be to sanctify the Whopper, to make it into a sacrament, but to attempt to influence our culture to make it more fitting for human beings bearing the image of God.

While our culture may not be holy, it should not be inhuman. This is the perspective we must bring to bear on all aspects of culture, especially on popular culture, which not only presents some unique challenges to personal piety, but which increasingly poses threats to our humanity.

F O U R

POPULAR CULTURE AND THE RESTLESS ONES

DON'T WORRY, BE HAPPY

If we cannot expect our culture to be a holy enterprise, we can at least try to avoid participating in its profanities. In a fallen world, sharing a common culture with those who do not honor God, we are still obliged to be obedient to God. Culture may be incapable of fulfilling the highest good; we must still choose to avoid its evil, and select from among greater and lesser goods.

The main question raised by popular culture concerns the most edifying way to spend one's time. If you and everyone in your family had to work sixteen hours a day, seven days a week, you would not have to ask whether or not you should plan your life around when "Entertainment Tonight" is scheduled. But most of us enjoy a level of leisure that leaves plenty of room for entertainment every night.

Sociologist Leo Lowenthal, writing in 1950, argued that the "basic dilemma concerning man's existence beyond the requirements of biological and material survival, the vital question of how to live out that stretch of life that is neither sleep nor work,"[1] was addressed in a very modern way as early as the sixteenth century. Lowenthal cites an essay by Montaigne, who was quite concerned about living in a world without faith. Some Americans tend to think that it wasn't until the 1962 Supreme

Court decision outlawing school prayer that secularization reared its ugly head. But skepticism as a social problem was very real for the generation that followed the Reformation.

While the doctrine of justification was the most substantive theological issue addressed by the Reformers, in the course of raising the issue of salvation they also necessarily raised questions about the relative authority of the Bible, the church, and individual conscience. If the church was not an infallible authority, and if the Bible could be interpreted in various conflicting ways, how could a person know what was true? If devout and godly men disagreed on matters as central to Christianity as the meaning of salvation, how could the average layman be sure that they were right on even more fundamental matters, such as the very existence of God?

For the above-average layman, the situation was no better. In the 1560s, there was a republication in Latin of the skeptical writings of Sextus Empiricus (early third century), who "questioned the reliability of either the senses or reason to prove the existence of God."[2] If one could not rely on the church, reason, or the senses for certainty of the existence of God, and one knew that none of one's fellow citizens could either, what hope was there unless you were a saint gifted with a beatific vision?

For Montaigne, such a state of affairs led to religious doubt, which in turn led to what we would call despair. Like many twentieth-century intellectuals (and nonintellectuals for that matter), facing a world without faith and without God, Montaigne suggested finding some means of near-perpetual distraction as an escape from the horror of cosmic isolation. "Variety," he wrote, "always solaces, dissolves, and scatters. . . . By changing place, occupation, company, I escape into the crowd of other thoughts and diversions, where it loses my trace, and leaves me safe."[3]

Montaigne probably would have been the first in his neighborhood with a satellite dish to pick up zillions of television stations. Such a level of diversion would have rendered him totally "safe."

A century later, Blaise Pascal saw the effects of the restlessness that had developed in the intervening years, as religion exerted less and less influence in people's lives. Writing in the seventeenth century, well before the Industrial Revolution and the rise of the "leisure class," and long before the perpetual blandishments of advertising, Pascal lamented (in his *Pensées*) the way people frittered their lives away with relatively trivial pursuits:

> Men are entrusted from infancy with the care of their honor, their property, their friends, and even with the property and the honor of their friends. They are overwhelmed with business, with the study of languages, and with physical exercises; and they are made to understand that they cannot be happy unless their health, their honor, their fortune and that of their good friends be in good condition, and that a single thing wanting will make them unhappy. Thus they are given cares and business which make them bustle about from break of day. — It is, you will exclaim, a strange way to make them happy! What more could be done to make them miserable? — Indeed! what could be done? We should only have to relieve them from all these cares; for then they would see themselves: they would reflect on what they are, whence they came, whither they go, and thus we cannot employ and divert them too much. And this is why, after having given them to so much business, we advise them, if they have some time for relaxation, to employ it in amusement, in play, and to be always fully occupied.
>
> How hollow and full of ribaldry is the heart of man![4]

Pascal concluded that "all the unhappiness of men arises from one single fact, that they cannot stay quietly in their own chamber. . . . They have a secret instinct which impels them to seek amusement and occupation abroad, and which arises from the sense of their constant unhappiness."

For Montaigne the skeptic, leisure (in Leo Lowenthal's phrase) "guarantees survival," while for the pious Pascal it "means self-destruction." One could conclude, as Lowenthal does, that the debate about the personal and social effects of popular culture is simply the latest chapter in a tale as old as human nature itself, or at least as old as *fallen* human nature, the nature that compelled Adam to hide from God rather than face up to Him in the Garden.

SOMETHING NEW UNDER THE SUN

But there *is* something new about popular culture. Modern popular culture is not just the latest in a series of diversions. It is rather a *culture of diversion*. One of the novelties of our present situation is the fact that such a large proportion of the population can spend such a large proportion of its time seeking diversion. The forty-hour week is a novelty in human history, as is the percentage of discretionary income enjoyed by a majority of Americans. Thanks to the blessing of the welfare state, even many of those surviving below the poverty level have more leisure time than did people similarly situated as little as 50 years ago.

Might it not be the case that when a society reaches a critical mass of leisure time, something in that society changes? Can the pursuit of entertainment by more and more people more and more of the time eventually affect the quality of life in society as a whole?

In addition to the problem of numbers, the popular culture of our age also boasts a great new machine, an engine of distraction, an entertainment appliance that brings to every home (even to every car) an unprecedented means of escape, a personal, one-eyed, electronic genie dedicated to solace, dissolve, and scatter. For a few hundred dollars and the painless connection of a coaxial cable, one can find a plenitude of diversion that would have exhausted even a Montaigne.

In the twentieth century (and into the twenty-first), Western nations possess social arrangements and technical possibilities that make modern popular culture a qualitatively different thing from any previous cultural phenomenon, even though it may serve for *individuals* exactly the same function of diverting attention away from asking about the origin and destiny of life. To understand popular culture in its natural habitat, we need to look at how it grew out of and transformed a number of other trends in modern society and in modern thought.

THE CRITIQUE FROM THE LEFT

A very superficial familiarity with popular culture would trace its origin to capitalism. It is easy to see how popular culture could be regarded as the people's mass-marketed Valium: a mass-produced, brand-name sedative that distracted the proletariat from the realities of its oppression. Consider this quote from a leftist critic of popular culture:

> Mass Culture is imposed from above. It is fabricated by technicians hired by businessmen; its audiences are passive consumers, their participation limited to the choice between buying and not buying. The Lords of *kitsch*,[5] in short, exploit the cultural needs of the masses in order to make a profit and/or to maintain their class rule.[6]

If he had stopped there, one might have assumed that Dwight Macdonald blamed capitalism for popular culture's inadequacies. But he concludes the sentence: " — in Communist countries, only the second purpose [class rule] obtains." In other words, Macdonald the leftist was as critical of the popular culture fostered by Stalin's regime as he was by that generated by Wall Street, Madison Avenue, and Sunset Boulevard.

Many of Macdonald's fellow leftists, while critical of American popular culture, realized that capitalism was not to blame for its follies. They knew that a principle applicable to many modern cultural phenomena also applied to popular culture (as Peter L. Berger has pointed out): what is often blamed on capitalism is really a function of that much more elusive social force, *modernity*.[7]

The terms *modernity* and *modernism* are overlapping, if not quite synonymous, labels for a host of social and cultural patterns that distinguish modern times. *Modernity* tends to be used in reference to sociological phenomena in industrialized, secularized societies, phenomena that are the unintentional result of social arrangements which differ sharply from those found in traditional societies. The term *modernity* is also applied to those changes in habits of thinking and feeling, the changes in the mood of a society, that often accompany social change.

Modernism, on the other hand, is usually used to describe a very self-conscious effort by the shapers of culture — mostly artists of one form or another — to rethink and recast their own deliberate activities in the wake of modernity.

Let me try to tell the story very simply. Once upon a time technology gave us many new machines, machines to produce things in large quantity and machines to transport things (and people) over large distances. This resulted in changes in how business was conducted, how families stayed together (or failed to), and how communities and nations interacted with each other and with their leaders. Those changes, in turn, resulted in different attitudes *unconsciously assumed by most of the populace* toward commerce, family, community, governments, and time and space itself. (Ironically, it makes a lot of sense to call all those things that are unconsciously assumed by people part of their *consciousness*.) That new state of affairs was labeled an effect of *modernity*.

Meanwhile, painters and composers and novelists and poets sensed the change in consciousness that was all around them. They anticipated new possibilities, new rhythms, new intimacies between man and machine, new perspectives on space and time (which are, after all, the basic raw materials for artists), and they *decided* to change how they did what they did *because* of this new world. Their collective cultural choices were soon labeled *modernism*.[8] Marshall Berman has related modernity and self-conscious modernism this way:

> To be modern is to experience personal and social life as a maelstrom, to find one's world and oneself in perpetual disintegration and renewal, trouble and anguish, ambiguity and contradiction: to be part of a universe in which all that is solid melts into air. To be a modern*ist* is to make oneself somehow at home in the maelstrom, to make its rhythms one's own, to move within its currents in search of the forms of reality, of beauty, of justice, that its fervid and perilous flow allows.[9]

Note that Berman qualifies the search for what used to be considered absolutes; reality, beauty, and justice are limited by what the ever-shifting setting of modernity will allow.

Popular culture was not simply *influenced* by, but was *created* by the same forces that resulted in modernity. In addition, as those forces created a change in consciousness in society, popular culture adapted to suit newly emerging desires, frustrations, and opportunities. Many of the attributes acquired by popular culture in its earliest forms continue to characterize it today. While the media have changed and stars have come and gone, the role that popular culture plays in our lives remains essentially the same, with one significant exception: *popular culture, especially in the past twenty-five years, has become a more dominant cultural force than ever before.*

This increasing influence has come at the expense of both high and folk culture, and has some special significance to Christians which will become clearer in the coming chapters. For the present, it should simply be noted that religion can be mediated through any kind of culture: high, folk, or popular. But of the three forms, only popular culture is truly a modern phenomenon. High culture has its roots in antiquity, in an age of conviction about absolutes, about truth, about virtue. However corrupted it has become over the centuries (and it has become quite corrupted in our own century), its essential features make it capable of maintaining and transmitting more about human experience in creation, and about God's redemptive intervention in history, than its alternatives.

Folk culture, while simpler in manner and less communicable from one folk to another, has the virtues of honesty, integrity, commitment to tradition, and perseverance in the face of opposition. Negro spirituals are one of our country's best examples of folk culture that retains essential religious truths over the long haul.

Popular culture, on the other hand, has some serious liabilities that it has inherited from its origins in distinctively modern, *secularized* movements. If we are in fact moving into an era more and more dominated by popular culture (often with the assistance of the institutional church), we must become more and more alert to those liabilities. The *consciousness* of popular culture, the manners and emotional habits it encourages us to take for granted, will become the consciousness of the society at large, the environment in which we are striving to be and to make disciples. To understand what this may mean, we need to take a closer look at how the spirit of popular culture has been created.

HOW YOU GONNA KEEP 'EM DOWN ON THE FARM AFTER THEY'VE SEEN THE FARM?

Popular culture was created by modernity. In turn, the greatest force shaping modernity was the Industrial Revolution. The new capacities for production by mechanized systems brought incredible changes to Western culture, just as they continue to transform newly industrialized non-Western cultures. The age of industry meant an unprecedented alleviation of poverty. More people could live with more material comfort than ever before. Goods that were once regarded as luxuries for the privileged few soon were considered necessities for the masses. One of those luxuries was leisure, now enjoyed to a greater extent by a larger proportion of the population than ever before.

But this economic growth and the delivery of large new blocks of "free" time was not delivered without a significant surtax. One need not be a Marxist to recognize that the early stages of industrialism did not create an environment that was exactly "fulfilling" for all the workers. As Clement Greenberg put it, industrialized workers discovered "a new capacity for boredom."[10] Factories introduced an uncommon level of tedium to the lives of workers. A number of critics of popular culture have observed, along the lines that Jacques Barzun has suggested, that

industrial life required something that would compensate the toilers for their loss of individuality, of self-will and self-regard, of free movement and dramatic effort. Something, I say, had to be done to palliate their nervous fatigue, their self-contempt, and their boredom, which is only vital energy unused. The tedium (if I may further improve a phrase) is the massage. And the compensation is the culture of cities, rooted in the newspaper and rising by degrees to spectator sports, organized betting, and panoptical sexuality.[11]

If these workers had been in the villages and small towns from which they came, they might have relieved the tedium by enjoying the pleasures afforded by activities rooted in folk culture: barn dances, play with extended family, traditional music, storytelling, hunting and fishing. But those traditional forms didn't fit in the city. For one thing, the community out of which such experiences grew and through which they subsisted did not exist in the new urban environment. Such activities were not just entertainment: they were part of a way of life that did not survive in the cities.

The more tedious industrial work became, the more desperate the search for diversion. Working on a farm can be laborious, but at least it allows interaction with living, growing, changing things. Working in a factory (especially prior to any significant forms of automation) was deadly dull by comparison. So, says Ernest van den Haag, "recreation" became "a search for excitement — vicarious or direct — to offset the monotony of work and give a feeling of 'living.' But excitement pursued for its own sake only exhausts eagerness and impulse without creating anything."12

If one is relying on popular culture to stimulate excitement, one will gradually require greater and greater levels of stimulation to achieve the same level of excitement. The makers of popular culture will gladly oblige. Since it is the purpose of most forms of popular culture to provide exciting distraction, we should not be surprised that over time, television programs, popular music, and other forms become more extreme (and more offensive) in their pursuit of titillation. Folk culture has the capacity to limit its extremes, since it is the expression of the values and aspirations of a community. Popular culture, on the other hand, presupposes the absence of a community of belief or conviction. It is for many a means of escape from such a community. Many teenagers have listened to their favorite radio station as a means of asserting their independence from their family. In fact, part of the excitement may come from the fact that the music is *their* music, not their parents'.

This aspect of popular culture is recognized by its defenders. Sociologist Herbert Gans praises the opportunities offered by popular culture for "Middle America": "Many working and even middle-class Americans are still in the process of liberating themselves from traditional parental cultures and learning how to be individuals with their own needs and values."[13] Gans goes on to say that popular culture in the form of popular magazines can work wonders for people eager to define themselves outside of any preexisting context.

Note that he is not talking about young people improving on the tastes of their parents, listening to a local symphony instead of Lawrence Welk, or hanging Picasso prints on their walls instead of velvet paintings of wide-eyed children. His escapees are not escaping from a lower culture to a higher one or an inferior one to a better one. In fact, he assumes they are remaining in the same "taste culture," as he calls it, but using popular cultural means to reject their parents' *values*.

One of the examples he uses is that of a young woman: "the spate of women's liberation articles in popular women's magazines helps a woman still deeply immersed in a male-dominated society to find ideas and feelings that allow her to start to struggle for her own freedom."[14] Gans shows no sense that such individualism is anything less than virtuous. After all, it's the American way to abandon your parents' values, especially if they seem at all inhibiting.

There is a much darker side to the use of popular culture to relieve boredom. Ernest Van den Haag has asked the question, "Who is slain when time is killed?" His answer implies that when we kill time, we are really killing ourselves. If there is a fundamental lack of fulfillment in our lives, a pall of tedium hangs over everything we do. "Diversion, however frantic, can overwhelm temporarily but not ultimately relieve the boredom which oozes from nonfulfillment."[15] One thinks of Montaigne, striving to fill his life with diversion, hoping to stave off the despair of life without God. Modernity has not excluded God from the universe. It has simply made it more difficult to maintain a consciousness of God's presence in a culture that increasingly ignores Him.

Modernity serves, ironically, as a compelling witness to

God, as it can present in stark contrast the difference between life with God and life apart from Him. In traditional societies one could enjoy relief from the oppression of meaninglessness under the sacred canopy of publicly professed faith. Even if you had no faith yourself, you could take comfort in the presence of those who did and in the order imparted to social existence by shared belief. But in modern secular cultures, the ooze of boredom is not so easily stanched.

This is one of the insights of satirical comedians like those on "Saturday Night Live," "Monty Python," or the old SCTV troupe. They borrow conventions from the entertainment world (Bill Murray's lounge crooner, Eric Idle's sleazy television announcer) to demonstrate how vacuous popular culture's attempt to escape vacuousness really is. But a steady diet of such astute humor merely takes us to a third level of emptiness.

Van den Haag was writing at a time when the topic of *ennui* was very fashionable. Deep, depressing boredom was still seen as a social problem, in part because the culture at large was unwilling to make the leap to accept the meaninglessness the philosophers had diagnosed. Ennui is no longer in vogue as a topic of serious conversation, in part because of the decline of serious conversation, in part because popular culture discovered how to make fun of ennui. Woody Allen's films, for example, are brilliant exercises in what Allan Bloom calls "nihilism with a happy ending."

But when Van den Haag was writing in the late 1950s, such dark giddiness was not a popular commodity. One could still take despair seriously. He pointed out that popular culture is unable to relieve restless boredom that springs from spiritual emptiness, since "diversion at most, through weariness and fatigue, can numb and distract anxiety."

Though the bored person hungers for things to happen to him, the disheartening fact is that when they do he empties them of the very meaning he unconsciously yearns for by using them as distractions. In popular culture even the second coming would become just another barren "thrill" to be watched on television till Milton Berle comes on. No distraction can cure boredom, just as the company so unceasingly pursued cannot stave off loneliness. The bored person is lonely for himself, not, as he thinks, for others. He misses the individuality, the capacity for experience from which he is debarred. No distraction can restore it. Hence he goes unrelieved and insatiable.[16]

Van den Haag's terminally bored consumer of popular culture is deprived of individuality because he has been cut off from the sources of understanding himself. Traditionally, the values and religious commitments of family and community provided the context for a person to experience his own individuality. Cut off from family and community by the mobility and impersonality of industrialized life, there is a new urgent necessity to "find" oneself. There is no community in the masses, only, in David Riesman's famous phrase, the "lonely crowd." As Dwight Macdonald has pointed out, in a traditional community the individual "is at once more important as an individual than in mass society and at the same time more closely integrated into the community, his creativity nourished by a rich combination of individualism and communalism. (The great culture-bearing elites of the past have been communities of this kind.)"[17]

But family and community are only media of meaning, not the source. High culture is another medium of meaning, one we'll explore in more detail in the following chapters. The transcendent reality of God Himself, and the experience of fellowship with Him in Christ, is the *source* of meaning. The question remains whether popular culture can serve as an able medium of meaning, or whether it is instead a distraction from confronting meaning, as well as meaninglessness.

THY HEADLINES ARE NEW EVERY MORNING

From its roots in early industrialized society, popular culture inherited two attributes that still characterize it: the quest for novelty, and the desire for instant gratification. The quest for novelty is not simply a search for new distractions; it involves the notion that a new thing will be better than the old one.

Advertisers rely on and cultivate this sensibility, although in recent years phrases such as "country-style" or "home-style" have crept into more and more ad copy, a recognition that consumers still have some lingering hankering for traditional tastes.

Daniel Bell has pointed out that modernism has changed our society's understanding of the very purpose of its high culture. High culture is now in the business of looking for new things, rather than, as in the past,

> setting a norm and affirming a moral philosophic tradition against which the new could be measured and (more often than not) censured. Indeed, society has done more than passively accept innovation; it has provided a market which eagerly gobbles up the new, because it believes it to be superior in value to all older forms. Thus, our culture has an unprecedented mission: it is an official, ceaseless search for a new sensibility.[18]

Of course, high culture is simply doing now what popular culture always did. This is why, as we shall see later, it was so easy for popular culture to displace high culture. Once high culture gave up the duty of sustaining the highest and best things that had been thought and written in the past, it was competing on the terms of popular culture, and it was no match.

Why did the quest for novelty become the norm? "How has it come about," C. S. Lewis once asked, "that we use the highly emotive word 'stagnation,' with all its malodorous and malarial overtones, for what other ages would have called 'permanence'?" It is, Lewis suggests, because the dominance of the machine in our culture altered our imagination. It gave us a "new archetypal image."

> It is the image of old machines being superseded by new and better ones. For in the world of machines the new most often really is better and the primitive really is the clumsy. And this image, potent in all our minds, reigns almost without rival in the minds of the uneducated. For to them, after their marriage and the births of their children, the very milestones of

life are technical advances. From the old push-bike and thence to the little car; from gramophone to radio and from radio to television; from the range to the stove; these are the very stages of their pilgrimage.[19]

Lewis goes on to say that this unconscious conviction that the new is therefore better is the greatest difference between modern men and women and their premodern ancestors. The notion that "the attainment of goods we have never yet had, rather than the defence and conservation of those we have already, is the cardinal business of life would most shock and bewilder them" if they could somehow visit our age.

If our desire for the new were limited to machines, it would not be a great tragedy. But a thirst for novelty, once ingrained, is not so easily quenched. We look for the new in everything. Our frenetic search for novelty is, says Daniel J. Boorstin, one of the signs that we demand "more than the world can give us."[20] Having seen so much change, having experienced so many new things, we assume that the storehouse for new things and new experiences is limitless.

We are especially keen to acquire new information (which is not the same thing as knowledge). We watch the evening network news to find out what happened during the day, we watch the 11:00 news to see if anything happened while we were watching something else, we watch the network "Have a Nice Day Morning Programs" to find out what happened overnight and what might happen today. We can also watch specialized "news" programs about the entertainment world, about financial and economic developments, about sports, even about the weather. T. S. Eliot's lament in Choruses from "The Rock" seems a sacrilege in the land of the Shrine of Infotainment:

> *Where is the Life we have lost in living?*
> *Where is the wisdom we have lost in knowledge?*
> *Where is the knowledge we have lost in information?*
> *The cycles of Heaven in twenty centuries*
> *Bring us farther from GOD and nearer to the Dust.*[21]

The constant quest for novelty can be extremely addictive, and it can easily obscure reflection on eternal realities and claims. But of course, as Montaigne understood, that is part of its purpose. If it is too painful to set your mind on the higher things, the allure of novelty makes distraction that much easier.

WHEN DO WE WANT IT? NOW!!

Not only did modernity impart to popular culture a preoccupation with the new, it also created a taste for the new *now*. Daniel Bell believes that "the greatest single engine in the destruction of the Protestant ethic was the invention of the installment plan, or instant credit. Previously one had to save in order to buy. But with credit cards one could indulge in instant gratification."[22] Once you could pay for something right away (or at least pretend you did), obtaining it instantly was simply a technical matter to be overcome by Yankee ingenuity.

Television is often accused of reducing the attention span of viewers. But television can't take the blame for the fact that modern people are impatient people. Much of our technology exists to mollify our impatience. We have near instantaneous access to information provided by computers and fax machines. We can communicate with friends and businesses by telephone rather than writing letters and waiting for responses. We can have most commodities delivered to our doorstep in hours rather than days or weeks via overnight courier services. Drive-thru food service has replaced drive-in restaurants. Don't even bother turning off the engine — just get back on the highway and eat on the way. If we want to enjoy the relative novelty of a meal at home, residents of most cities and suburbs can now shop for groceries twenty-four hours a day. When we get home, we need not wait to prepare it, since frozen food and microwaves eliminate the necessity of anything resembling cooking.

If we don't have the cash for something we want to buy, we don't have to wait for banks to open : automatic teller machines (linked on national networks) give us our money (even borrowed money) in seconds. The relationship of time and space has been altered with modern transportation; while few of us ever take the Concorde, all of us get aggravated if traffic causes us any delays, and speed limits are regarded as suggested minimum velocities rather than a maximum threshhold.

In this cultural context, television's pace might just as easily be seen as an *effect* of impatience and short attention spans as much as a cause. *USA Today*, not so affectionately dubbed "McPaper" by many journalists, was accused when it first appeared of capitulating to the quick and dirty spirit of television journalism; its distinctive vending boxes even looked like television sets. But television is just a part of the cycle of our culture's habit of hurry. While not innocent, television, the most significant medium of modern mass culture, should not take the rap alone.

The pursuit of the new and the now is evident in the structure and programming of popular culture's most significant medium: television. It is also evident, as we shall see in a later chapter, in popular culture's most dominant idiom: rock 'n' roll. Although rock pays homage to "oldies," the culture of rock could not survive on its "classics." Moreover, the aesthetic of rock music also stresses immediacy in all senses of the word.

POPULAR CULTURE AND THE L WORD

Early mass culture was secularized from the very beginning. Since it catered to an audience that was not homogeneous in religious conviction, it tended to avoid any reference to religion except in the vaguest, blandest manner. Folk culture, on the other hand, is tied to a particular people, with traditions that include religious convictions; so it almost always has some religious connection, either in subject matter (stories from the Bible or about personal religious experience), or by virtue of where the culture was shared (e.g., church meetings), or both.

As industrialized populations became more and more mobile, the ties to family and community became weaker and weaker. The sense that every individual person had a place of belonging within a family or the society of a community was soon lost. Of course, many people were willing (as many still are) to give this up voluntarily. Many people were eager to be liberated from the strictures of traditional society. The city beckoned as a place of liberation, where one could find oneself because one could lose oneself in the crowd.

In addition to the social and spiritual effects of such deliberate dislocation, the loss of normative guidance from family and community created a vacuum that popular culture (especially in the form of popular journalism) was more than willing to fill. In time, especially for the young, standards of dress, of manners, of conversation, of friendship and love, and even of belief came to be shaped by popular culture more than by family, church, or community.

Of course, another way of interpreting the standard-generating power of popular culture is to say that in a liberal (that is, individualistic and egalitarian) society, people are free to choose for themselves among various standards presented by family, church, community, or popular culture in the form of magazines, movies, and music of the day. But that way of phrasing it is a bit like saying that an election is no less fair just because one candidate bribed a significant portion of the electorate to vote for him. After all, they *could* have voted for the other guy if they really wanted to.

Ethical norms prescribed by traditional sources such as family and religion contain an implicit threat that you will be punished in some way if you do not behave properly. Popular culture's moral guidance, on the other hand, whether from Donahue, *Cosmopolitan*, or Def Leppard, contains the tacit message that *you* can choose, *you* are the master of your fate, *you* are the final arbiter in setting your standards, and *you* deserve a break today: after all, like Cybill Shepherd, you're *worth* it. Your parents and your pastor never left you with that impression.

This invitation to moral autonomy is like a powerful bribe offered by popular culture. And what does it have to lose? Absolutely nothing. In fact, if you accept the bribe, you'll *give* them money, either by buying their product or by watching their program. Neat.

If originally called into being by the industrialism that also created modernity, popular culture has subsequently tapped into one of the great modern philosophies: Liberalism.

Every form of cultural expression builds on something else. In high culture, artists (at least those worth paying attention to) work within a tradition. Even the proponents of the avant-garde were extremely concerned about all that had gone before it; the great avant-garde artists (Eliot, Stravinsky, Picasso) were haunted by tradition. Folk culture has a more direct and organic tie to tradition.

Popular culture, too, must build on something, if for no other reason than that it needs some raw materials. Up until the last decade or two, popular culture has tended to rely on high culture and folk culture for its raw material. Writing in 1939, Clement Greenberg rather resented popular culture's habit of looting high culture: "It borrows from it devices, tricks, stratagems, rules of thumb, themes, converts them into a system, and discards the rest. It draws its life blood, so to speak, from this reservoir of accumulated experience."[23] Walt Disney was a genius at such plundering. Long before Mickey Mouse was conducting Moussorgsky's "Night on Bald Mountain" in Fantasia, Disney had Madame Clara Cluck, a stout and stuffy diva, performing (and spoofing) arias from Puccini and Verdi.

But in addition to snitching a few cultural artifacts here and there as raw material, popular culture excels at shoplifing in the marketplace of ideas. Adaptive parasite that it is, popular culture has been able to assimilate elements of such philosophical fashions as Rationalism, Romanticism, Utilitarianism, Relativism, Nihilism, and Postmoderism, usually in a relatively benign form. Much of what these have imparted to popular culture remains.

SOMETHING COMPLETELY DIFFERENT

I remember the first time I encountered the work of the English comedy group Monty Python. I had just finished a course in modern drama, studying Brecht, Ionesco, Pinter, Beckett, and Antonin Artaud, the genius of what was called "the theatre of cruelty." John Cleese, Eric Idle, and their chums amazed me with their ability to combine those modern dramatic conventions with the English music hall tradition and schtick from the BBC.

If popular culture can squeeze some laughs out of a moral

goon like Artaud, it should have no problem getting mileage out of a much friendlier philosophy like Liberalism.

Liberalism is *the* modern philosophy. It is also, in a way, the most ancient. It has the echo of a very early temptation to it. For, as Jacques Barzun has defined it, Liberalism is

> an assertion of the primacy of Man. Man must be free to fashion his life and his institutions in the light of his ever-expanding intellect. Hence all the old repressive arrangements must be destroyed — kings and priests, inherited traditions and unexamined creeds. Custom law must be recast by reason into a code, parliaments must be set up as the arena of free discussion; in theory, nothing is sacred, nothing beyond the reach of questioning and remaking. Liberalism makes Man his own master.[24]

Not only is man his own master — *every* man is *his* own master. This accords quite nicely with the structure of popular culture, in which what is *popular* determines what is "good." The People's Choice awards in Hollywood, for example, reward not intrinsic merit, but sheer popularity.

The individualism of Liberalism not only *liberates* people from each other, it necessarily *isolates* them. A thoroughgoing individualism, which acknowledges no binding ties to family or community, leads to loneliness as well as autonomy. Popular culture may seem to be something that overcomes this isolation; after all, listening to popular music or watching a favorite television program can be a point of shared experience.

But it can as easily work the other way. Many of us have had the experience of meeting TV zombies, people who cannot wrench themselves from the set when someone is in the room. In fact, at one time or another, most of us (under certain conditions) have *been* TV zombies. Ernest Van den Haag is very pessimistic about the possibility of popular culture (especially mass media) to overcome chronic individualism:

> All mass media in the end alienate people from personal experience and, though appearing to offset it, intensify their

moral isolation from each other, from reality and from themselves. One may turn to the mass media when lonely or bored. But mass media, once they become a habit, impair the capacity for meaningful experience. Though more diffuse and not as gripping, the habit feeds on itself, establishing a vicious circle as addictions do.[25]

It would seem that the differentiating factor is whether or not participating in a particular aspect of popular culture is habitual or deliberate behavior. The more habitual it is, the less likely it is to promote shared experience.

One of the problems with popular culture is that, *by itself*, it does not teach the sort of habits necessary to enjoy it wisely. Unless you had a taste for something better, you would never get tired of eating fast food or frozen dinners all of the time. If you were dissatisfied with such a diet, you wouldn't be able to define your dissatisfaction unless you had something else to compare it with.

Popular culture used to live in the shadow of high culture. It was once generally recognized by the custodians of culture (including artists, teachers, and preachers) that popular culture was an inferior form. Popular culture was seen as something fleeting and disposable, but most people acknowledged that something more permanent was available elsewhere, even if they didn't much care for it themselves.

Since the 1960s, the aesthetics of popular culture have effectively displaced those of high culture. As serious artists became less and less confident that there *were* any higher or permanent values they could represent in their work, popular culture's pursuit of ephemeral fun came to dominate high culture as well. Popular culture doesn't "look up" to anything today; it simply looks back at its own past. Once popular culture paid homage to high culture (e.g., the classical music used in *Fantasia*); today it is fascinated with the popular culture of the past. In fact, the roles have become reversed: while popular culture ignores high culture, the institutions once committed to the preservation of high culture are obsessed with popular culture. It would not have been surprising to find TV comedians such as

Steve Allen or Sid Caesar incorporating bits into their routines that had been inspired by Shakespeare. Today's comedians ignore the classics, while in university English departments dissertations are being presented and symposia convened on "The Honeymooners" or the lyrics of Paul McCartney. High culture once served (at least for those with some education) as a point of reference for the enjoyment of popular culture. It is now almost unknown.

The story of how this turnabout happened is an important one for understanding the place of popular culture in our society, and it's one we will examine. But first, in the next two chapters, we'll compare the aesthetic capacities and methods of traditional high culture with those of popular culture. For the difference between the two forms is not simply a matter of class or taste, but reflects different ways of understanding creation and one's place in it.

ACCOUNTING FOR TASTE

BUT IS IT ART?

If you are a student of popular culture, you are familiar with periodicals such as *Journal of Popular Culture, Cultural Critique, Cultural Notebooks,* and *Representations.* In such publications there is a rather predictable range of articles. There are studies that are content analyses: "Your Cheatin' Heart: Infidelity and the Dilemma of Reconciliation in Country Music Lyrics," "Mary Poppins Was a Witch: Proto-New Age Mysticism in Disney Films, 1960-1980." There will be some articles that analyze style: "Krazy Kat and Dick Tracy: Two Modes of Surrealism in Comic Strips," "German Expressionism in the Films of Busby Berkeley." And there will be a lot of articles emphasizing political concerns: "Gender and Work: The Images of Nurses in Television Drama," "Black and Blue Collar: Race and the Working Class in Popular Fiction."[1]

What you are not likely to find in such periodicals, or in classes on popular culture at colleges and universities, is much in the way of assessment of the *artistic* attributes of popular culture, although such analysis may be found in courses in film, literature, or music that focus on popular works. Most scholars working within the discipline of popular culture (or "cultural studies," as it is often called) are much more concerned about political questions concerning race, gender, and class than about matters of aesthetic quality. In fact, they tend to regard aesthetic judgment as totally determined by political concerns, working with the quasi-Marxist assumption that matters of taste and aesthetic judgment are determined by social class.

Scholars in this field, as one writer put it, "take as their subject the intersection of culture and politics, examining such questions as how certain cultural artifacts — works of literature, say — are 'produced' and 'consumed,' or how and why some things come to be regarded as 'high culture' and some as 'popular culture.'"[2]

From a Christian perspective, restricting the study of popular culture in such a way is extremely inadequate. Certainly, we must be concerned with the social aspects of culture, but we should be concerned as much about the *nature* and the *effects* of cultural phenomena as about their *cause*, and we *certainly* cannot argue that political and economic forces are *ultimate* in the shaping of culture. If, for example, a particular cultural form encourages the sort of individualism that presupposes that you have to discover who you are independent of family and community, we have to regard it as problematic.

HABITS OF THE HEART

Just as we cannot reduce the study of culture to questions of the distribution of political power, so we cannot reduce it to questions of social behavior. This, unfortunately, is a common approach among Christians who worry that the content of popular culture will encourage certain behavior (e.g., disrespect to parents, drug abuse, sexual promiscuity, proclivity to violence, etc.). While these are obviously legitimate concerns, what should attract more attention is the effect of consistent exposure to popular culture, whether or not the content is objectionable, on the development of internal dispositions. The habits of mind, heart, and soul — in short the qualities of *character* — that are encouraged or discouraged by the aesthetic dynamics of our cultural activities are at least as important to Christian reflection on culture as are social considerations. After all, we believe that a person *does* what a person *is*, not the other way around — that who we are inside is ultimately more significant than who we are outside.

In an age of egalitarianism and relativism, it is easier than ever to regard matters of taste as wholly private and personal. I like Bach, you like Bon Jovi, praise the Lord anyhow. But is aesthetic judgment purely a subjective and neutral matter? Is "beauty" exclusively in the eye of the beholder? Is something "beautiful" just because I like it, or does it have some objective quality rooted in creation that allows me to *recognize* that it is beautiful?

When I say I "like" Bach, and you say you "like" Bon Jovi, are we really using the same verb? That is, when I listen to Bach and you listen to Bon Jovi, is essentially the same thing happening to each of us? At one level, all we mean is that each of us takes pleasure in listening to our respective music. But there are many ways of taking pleasure, not all of them comparable, and not all of them morally good. One person may take pleasure in visiting the elderly in nursing homes on Saturday afternoons; another may take pleasure in mugging old ladies on the street on Saturday nights. One person has a "taste" for acts of benevolence, another for acts of violence. But this difference in preference is not simply a matter of "taste" as the word is usually used.

Is the pleasure taken in listening to Bach essentially the same as the pleasure taken in listening to Bon Jovi? In other words, is it simply a matter of "personal taste"? (I am reminded of the joke about the anthropologist, a thoroughgoing cultural relativist, who insisted that cannibalism was simply a matter of taste until he found himself on the cannibals' menu and suddenly enjoyed a conversion to a belief in moral absolutes.)

If what happens when we listen to classical music, read literature, or attend the theater is fundamentally a different kind of experience from listening to rock 'n' roll, reading romance novels, or watching "The Cosby Show," then it is clear that having a "taste" for high culture is a very different matter from having a "taste" for popular culture.

Since our society is now more influenced by the ethos of popular culture than by the standards of high culture, it is likely that we ourselves are likewise affected, unless we are self-conscious and deliberate in selecting the cultural influences in our lives. In the rest of this chapter, we will look at the differences in the aesthetics of popular and high culture, and consider some of the theological and spiritual ramifications of those differences.

BOOKS AND BATTING AVERAGES

One of the reasons we often resist the making of aesthetic judgments is that the American spirit of egalitarianism is suspicious of anyone who asserts that their taste is objectively superior to those of the "masses." No loyal American wants to be a snob. After all, as de Tocqueville noted, Americans have a strong feeling for the moral authority of the majority.[3]

Another reason Americans are uncomfortable with evaluation of artistic merit is that we tend to prefer quantitative to qualitative reasoning. Dwight Macdonald has suggested that this may explain the American passion for sports and the relative apathy for the arts and letters. (Anyone who believes Americans are not distinctive in this matter should reflect on the fact that as of this writing one of the most popular French television programs is *Apostrophes*, a weekly seventy-five-minute show that features interviews with serious authors, all discussing a particular theme. Between two to six million viewers watch each week. The program has been on since 1974. Of course, the French are also the people who consider Jerry Lewis a serious artist.)

Unlike artistic performance, "the quality of performance in sports can be determined statistically." Macdonald points out that you can prove by appealing to batting averages that one ballplayer is a better hitter than another. There is no such statistic you can cite to demonstrate that one novelist is better than another. The assessing of performance in sports is scientific in nature; it "deals with measurable phenomena according to generally accepted rules." Literature, on the other hand, is not as easy to evaluate, though it is not impossible to make judgments. It is, as Macdonald explains, a much different process.

> This is a different operation involving an appeal — by reason, analysis, illustration, and rhetoric — to cultural values which critic and reader have in common, values no more susceptible of scientific statement than are the moral values-in-

common to which Jesus appealed but which, for all that, exist as vividly and definitely as do mercy, humility, and love.[4]

Aesthetic judgment is by nature more elusive than scientific method will allow. It requires patience, training, and a willingness to submit to our elders. It is very much like wisdom in that regard. Its virtues are incompatible with the American penchant for *practical* reason.

Since popular culture is designed to be immediately ours, apprehended without our having to cultivate any particular skills, sensibilities, or sensitivities, it is not surprising that very few critics have taken the time to try to understand the aesthetics of popular culture. One who has, at least in an introductory but helpful way, is Abraham Kaplan, who in 1966 published an essay in the *Journal of Aesthetics and Art Criticism* called "The Aesthetics of Popular Arts."

Kaplan begins by noting that most critics dismiss popular culture as being simple, unsophisticated, artless, flat, and lifeless. But, he insists, simplicity itself is not a vice. Think of the phrase "classic simplicity," and you realize that simplicity is in fact an aesthetic virtue. The best art is simple; it "strips away what is unessential."[5] He admits that we can condemn popular art for stripping away that which should remain, but that requires first that we establish what complexity is necessary and what is not.

Kaplan also says that the criticism that popular art is inferior because it is "standardized" misses the mark. Italian opera, Elizabethan farces, and Greek tragedy were standardized. The form of the sonata, the symphony, and the sonnet are all systems of standardization. So to criticize soap operas or Westerns or science fiction movies because they are standardized is unfair.

BAD FORM

The problem with standardized popular culture is that what is standardized wasn't very good in the first place. The stereotypes it followed are faulty. The inferiority of popular culture's "mass-produced" quality "is not that each instance of the type so closely resembles all the others, but that the type as a whole so little resembles anything outside of it."[6]

> Where the simplifications of great art show us human nature in its nakedness, the stereotypes of popular art strip away even the flesh, and the still, sad music of humanity is reduced to the rattle of dry bones. It is not simplification but schematization that is achieved; what is put before us is not the substance of the text but a reader's digest. All art selects what is significant and suppresses the trivial. But for popular art the criteria of significance are fixed by the needs of the standardization, by the editor of the digest and not by the Author of the reality to be grasped.[7]

This paragraph describes the essence of the aesthetic limitations of popular culture. Great art reveals something about human nature because it is forced to conform to created reality. It selects its material according to the demands of the "Author of the reality to be grasped," not according to the arbitrary needs imposed by marketing departments or Nielsen ratings. The television or record producer, the paperback editor or the movie production company is interested in discovering successful *formulas* and repeating them, not because they will better explore the content, but because the market is already there for such a production. Cop shows are hot and music videos are hot? Let's do a music video cop show. Nobody assumed that "Miami Vice" would be better suited to explore human nature because of the pastels and the popular tunes. "The Author of the reality to be grasped" wasn't consulted, because no one was concerned with the reality to be grasped, but only with a form/formula to be exploited for as long as the audience would buy it.

The structure of "Miami Vice" was certainly new when it first aired. The show had a gimmick, but the gimmick wore out very quickly, and the show wasn't hot any longer, its audience wanting a new gimmick. The important thing to remember is that it was the formula that made the show attractive. Kaplan argues that "popular art uses formulas, not for analysis, but for the experience itself."[8] A great novelist or playwright may also use formulas, but the formula is a utensil, not the meal.

Kaplan continues on this theme by commenting on the fact that popular culture cannot afford to disappoint our expectations too much. The audience of popular culture participates in it armed with a particular understanding of the way the world is, and does not expect to have that understanding seriously challenged.

> Both producer and consumer of popular art confine themselves to what fits into their own schemes, rather than omitting only what is unnecessary to the grasp of the scheme of things. The world of popular art is bounded by the limited horizons of what we think we know already; it is two-dimensional because we are determined to view it without budging a step from where we stand.[9]

Kaplan touches here on a theme that would seem to summarize the difference between *art* and *entertainment*. Entertainment reaches out to us where we are, puts on its show, and then leaves us essentially unchanged, if a bit poorer in time and money. It does not (and usually does not claim to) offer us any new perspective on our lives or on other matters in creation. Later in his essay Kaplan remarks that "a taste for popular art is a device for remaining in the same old world and assuring ourselves that we like it."[10]

THAT'S ENTERTAINMENT

Some stuffy critics seem to be disturbed by the fact that popular culture is entertaining. Kaplan says such objections miss an important point. *All* art, high or low, is *at least* entertaining. The problem with popular art is that it entertains in a very literal sense.

> We are entertained in the primary sense, when we are housed and fed, and not merely amused; popular art only makes us guests in our own home. This is to say that popular art is not, as is often supposed, a *diversion*, redirecting our interests, diverting them to other and more satisfying objects of interest. It does not arouse new interests but reinforces old

ones. Such satisfaction as it affords stems from the evocation in memory of past satisfactions, or even from remembered fantasies of fulfillment. What we enjoy is not the work of popular art but what it brings to mind. There is a nostalgia characteristic of the experience of popular art, not because the work as a form is familiar but because its very substance is familiarity. . . . The skill of the artist is not in providing an experience but in providing occasions for reliving one. The emotions that come into being are not *expressed* by his materials but are *associated* with them. They are not embodied in the object but are conveyed by it, transmitted. . . . In the experience of popular art we lose ourselves, not in a work of art but in the pools of memory stirred up.[11]

Television critic Tom Shales once remarked that "familiarity breeds contentment," and popular culture could not survive without familiarity. Popular culture begins and ends with the familiar. It "leaves our feelings essentially unchanged. . . . It neither transforms nor fulfills our desires but only reminds us of them."[12]

Good art, on the other hand, takes us to a world we wouldn't have imagined ourselves. It does not leave us where it found us. "In a fully aesthetic experience, feeling is deepened, given new content and meaning. Till then, we did not know what it was we felt; one could say that the feeling was not truly ours."[13] Great music, literature, painting, or architecture imprints itself in our lives and becomes a reference point for our most subtle and profound experiences.

GETTING TO KNOW YOU

Of course, such impressions do not come easily. I remember the first time I heard the music of Giovanni Gabrieli, a composer of the late sixteenth century. I was a junior in high school, and just beginning to get seriously interested in classical music. But *this* music was beyond me. After hearing a few canzoni for brass, I remarked to a more experienced friend, "This stuff all sounds alike." He appropriately rolled his eyes. About five years later, after having acquired a taste for the richness of Gabrieli and his contemporaries (but having forgotten how ignorant I once was), I played a recording of his music for brass for a young lady that I particularly wanted to impress with my sophisticated passion and *savoir-faire* (as well as my neat stereo system). As the reverberation of the final chord faded away, she looked at me inquisitively, asking, "Do many people like this sort of music?"

Well, perhaps not naturally. "To recognize that how much you get out of an art experience depends on how much you put into it is not moralistic but strictly aesthetic," asserts Kaplan.[14] But popular art will not allow too much being put into the experience. One wouldn't want to work too hard at listening to Barry Manilow, which is why more people like him than like Gabrieli. But one wonders if Manilow is as *well*-known as is old Giovanni? Kaplan argued that popular art cannot bear the sustained attention that high art can, so we remain well-acquainted with it; but the relationship is always superficial, never maturing into intimacy.[15] We may know all of the Beach Boys records by heart, but the liaison with their music may be comparable to a summer's fling with a Malibu surfer.

And just as with flings with surfers, so with popular culture: every summer we demand something new. But that new thing should have a certain familiarity about it. Somewhat paradoxically (but only somewhat), popular culture

> is characterized by a combination of novelty and repetition: the same beloved star appears in what can be described as a new role. The novelty whips up a flagging interest. At the same time the repetition minimizes the demands made on us: we can see at a glance what is going on, and we know already how it will all turn out.[16]

MORE THAN JUST A PRETTY FACE

Kaplan's reference to the star system brings up another attribute of popular culture that deserves some attention: celebrityism. Popular culture is more impersonal than folk culture for obvious reasons. It is more impersonal than high culture for the less than obvious reason that it fails to engage as much of our person in it. To put it another way, if we think we are fully engaged in popular culture ("I'm really into the Dead"), it is likely that there are parts of our person that we are cutting off or suppressing. But we have a *need* for the personal. Popular culture makes up for its impersonality by emphasizing the personality of the performers rather than the personal capacities of their work. "The individual buried in the mass audience can relate himself to the individual in the artist. . . . The artist is thus charismatic and his works become the expression of this charisma rather than, as in the past, objective creations."[17]

The amazing proliferation of television talk shows is testimony to the extent to which we demand to have popular culture celebrities display their personalities. "Gossip" or celebrity magazines aren't immediate enough: we want to see Bruce Willis or Madonna in the flesh, talking with other people. The talk show host isn't just an entertainer, he is our surrogate.

The feelings aroused by popular culture and, fittingly, displayed by its celebrities are often less than sincere. Kaplan says that sentimentality is one of the attributes of popular art, and reminds his readers that the dictionary meaning ("superficial, affected, spurious") is precisely right. It should be noted that many comedians in the past decade have gotten a lot of mileage out of mimicking the sentimentality of their colleagues in show business. With an air of mock mock sincerity, David Letterman and Paul Schaffer congratulate and praise one another five nights a week. Billy Crystal came from nowhere and became a star with three little words ("You look MAHvelous!") that spoofed the convention of affected behavior so common among his colleagues.

Sentimentality is as rampant in the culture of evangelicalism as it is in popular culture outside the church. Perhaps this is one of the reasons evangelicalism adapted itself to popular culture so readily. The friendliness of it, its lack of ambiguity, its sense of familiarity, its celebrityism — add to these qualities sentimentalism, and one realizes how much the two cultures have in common. But sentimentality may be the most corrupting of these qualities. Kaplan is eager to acknowledge that the object of sentimentality may be quite worthy — love of country, familial affection, grief at the loss of a friend — "but the feelings called forth spring too quickly and easily to acquire substance and depth. They are so lightly triggered that there is no chance to build up a significant emotional discharge."[18]

Kaplan quotes R. H. Blythe as saying that sentimentality is loving something more than God does. Like his criticism earlier that the selection of significant material in art relies on an objective standard in creation, so with the extent of emotion. The scale and proportion of emotion should be rooted in reality. In popular art, however, "the sentimentalist makes himself the standard of proportionality of feeling; the only meaning that matters to him is what he has stored up within."[19]

The subjectivism that is evident here is extremely important. It demonstrates that the individualism that characterizes the sort of *social structure* which gave rise to popular culture also characterizes its *aesthetic structure*. Just as modern individualism encourages each person to define their own *social* reality *apart from considerations about how the creation is ordered* (Should I get married or live with someone? Should I be heterosexual or homosexual? Should I believe in God or be an atheist? Should I be a faithful wife or a lesbian feminist?), so modern individualism encourages people to define their own *aesthetic* reality *apart from considerations about how the creation is ordered.*

I believe this is why people who don't watch television find it so "artificial" when occasionally exposed to it. Those of us who watch it often are accustomed to its conventions and its clichés and can "deal" with it. But do we thus have a harder time "dealing" with reality? If there is a disjunction between reality in the created order and popular culture, where do our sympathies lie? As Christians, of course we say they lie with creation. But is that a confession of our lips only? Is our understanding of love, of grief, of honor, of despair, of any human emotion more influenced by the stereotypical version of such experience in popular culture, or by life among real people?

THE GREAT ESCAPE

The problem of popular culture is not that it is escapist. It is that it is not escapist enough. J. R. R. Tolkien, in his famous essay "On Fairy-Stories," points out that there's nothing wrong *per se* with wanting to escape; we would praise such a desire in a prisoner of war. "Why should a man be scorned, if, finding himself in prison, he tries to get out and go home? Or if, when he cannot do so, he thinks and talks about other topics than jailers and prison-walls?" Critics must be wary, warned Tolkien, of confusing the "Escape of the Prisoner with the Flight of the Deserter."[20] The critical question is what one is escaping *from* and what one is escaping *to*. Kaplan suggests that popular art does not offer us enough of a world to receive us, because it is limited by our individualistic expectations.

> Popular art depicts the world, not as it is, nor even as it might be, but as we would have it. In that world we are neither strangers nor afraid, for it is of our own making. Everything in it is selected and placed in our interest. It is a world exhausted in a single perspective — our own — and it is peopled by cardboard figures that disappear when viewed edgewise. Art opens to us a landscape over which we may roam freely, unfolds events that can be seen through the eyes of even the least of their participants.[21]

This metaphor is very much like that used by Tolkien in "On Fairy-Stories," in which he talks about successful fantasy literature (the term we use today) creating a Secondary World, a place that is "real" though different from the Primary World available to our senses.

Of course, few works of popular culture are as bad as Kaplan's theory describes. After all, it is a theory that holds true generally speaking. If one defined what a work of high culture was, it would be impossible to find something that completely fulfilled all such criteria perfectly. The purpose of such theorizing is not to argue that no work of popular art has any redeeming value. There are numerous films, television programs, rock songs, or detective novels that are splendid productions as entertainment and as art.

Everything is permissible, but not everything is beneficial or constructive, says Paul in 1 Corinthians 10. Eating meat offered to idols is no problem for the Christian as long as the Christian doesn't believe that the idols have any spiritual reality. As long as the Corinthian believers were not caught up in the *Zeitgeist* of Corinth, as long as the sensibility of the culture did not dominate their own sensibilities, they could participate in the intrinsically innocent activities their culture afforded. But if someone was gripped by the culture's own myths, even the meat was tainted.

The same holds true in our day. There is nothing wrong with frivolous activity for one whose life is not committed to frivolity. There is no harm in superficial pleasures for one who also has a knowledge of the tragic and of the transcendent. The subjectivism of popular culture is impotent for someone whose life is characterized by a rootedness in objective reality.

Christians should not fear the idols and myths of our day, as long as they have no reverence for them. But idols and myths can take the form of moods and sensibilities as well as stone and creed, and there are many disturbing signs that many contemporary Christians have made the limited and limiting sensibility of popular culture their own. In the next chapter, we'll continue our examination of the aesthetics of popular culture by looking at a little-known work by C. S. Lewis.

BETTER TO RECEIVE

FOOD FOR THOUGHT

Let us do with food what we've been doing with culture in general (and art in particular) — let's separate three different "cultures" of the preparation and service of food: high (gourmet), folk (traditional home cooking), and popular (fast food). Just as with art, there will be food that fails to fit neatly into any one of these categories. My favorite pizza restaurant transcends all of them. Many ethnic foods are served fast-food style, but they come from traditional sources. But the categories work as a rough approximation of different food cultures.

Most people would agree that fast food has deficiencies that the other two categories do not, not simply in nutritional value or in taste, but in the *ethos*, the way the food is served, consumed, and experienced. Most young men of moderate means trying to make a positive impression on a young woman do *not* treat her to a meal at the nearest Burger King. They realize there is definitely something missing in the meal's social experience. Now, if every meal you ever ate was from a fast-food joint, would that affect your outlook on the meaning of meals? If there was never any elegance or grace, any ritual or decorum as part of your meals, if all the food you ever consumed was delivered to you by a person in a funny-looking hat, and was wrapped in cardboard or styrofoam, would that affect your impressions of the Biblical metaphor of the Marriage Supper of the Lamb?

The problem of popular culture is not the inadequacies of any one artifact, but the inadequacies of the whole, what might be called a cultural *gestalt*, the consciousness created by popular culture when it is unalleviated by values from traditional or high culture and by deliberate attention. "Why am I habitually turning on the radio in the car as soon as I buckle the seat belt?" "Why do I need background noise from the television set whenever I'm alone?" "Why do I always rent movies that are the cinematic equivalent of Twinkies?" Asking these initial questions is the first step in becoming conscious of the habits of careless restlessness which popular culture has infused in us. Developing a theory that demonstrates the deficiencies of popular culture should give any thinking person the initiative to take that first step.

ANOTHER EXPERIMENT

C. S. Lewis once mused on what a perfectly bad book would be like, and he ended up writing *An Experiment in Criticism*,[1] a virtually forgotten work that offers much wise counsel for attempts to understand popular culture.

In the book, Lewis set out to ask the same question we asked earlier, the question about whether the word "like" means the same thing when applied to Bach and to Bon Jovi (although one doubts that Professor Lewis would have troubled himself with Bon Jovi, had they been around in 1961; Perry Como perhaps). His goal was to come up with an alternative to the usual way literary critics distinguished between a good book and a bad book, and between good taste and bad taste. He wanted "to discover how far it might be plausible to define a good book as a book which is read in one way, and a bad book as a book which is read another."[2]

What marks the different ways of reading? Lewis lists four distinctions between what he calls "literary" and "unliterary" reading.

The sure mark of an unliterary man is that he considers "I've read it already" to be a conclusive argument against reading a work. . . . Those who read great works, on the other hand, will read the same work ten, twenty or thirty times during the course of their life.[3]

Lewis's second point is that unliterary readers generally "do not set much store by reading." Reading is something they do when there is nothing else to do, or to relieve boredom on a train, in a doctor's office, or on nights when they can't sleep. Literary people, on the other hand, "are always looking for leisure and silence in which to read and do so with their whole attention."[4]

The third distinction is that a book for the literary can be a deep, profound experience, "an experience so momentous that only experiences of love, religion, or bereavement can furnish a standard of comparison. Their whole consciousness is changed."[5]

Finally, "what they have read is constantly and prominently present to the mind" of "good" readers. They remember and savor favorite passages. "Scenes and characters from books provide them with a sort of iconography by which they interpret or sum up their experience." Unliterary readers "seldom think or talk about their reading."[6]

But Lewis is unimpressed with people who read all the "right books" because they are status seekers or "culture vultures." He also says that many people who deal with literature professionally are not very good readers. Lewis had the occasional colleague who didn't want to talk about literature "after hours." Books for them were a job, like bricks for a bricklayer, not a passion.

Lewis then goes on to compare how a similar set of distinctions could be made concerning the use of music and the visual arts. In both of these instances, as with literature, one can either "receive" a work of art or "use" it. To distinguish between the two, Lewis offers the following analogy:

A work of (whatever) art can be either "received" or "used." When we "receive" it we exert our senses and imagination and various other powers according to a pattern invented by the artist. When we "use" it we treat it as assistance for our own activities. The one, to use an old-fashioned image, is like being taken for a bicycle ride by a man who may know roads we have never yet explored. The other is like adding one of those little motor attachments to our own bicycle and then going for one of our familiar rides. These rides may in themselves be good, bad, or indifferent. The "uses" which the many make of the arts may or may not be intrinsically vulgar, depraved, or morbid. That's as may be. "Using" is inferior to "reception" because art, if used rather than received, merely facilitates, brightens, relieves or palliates our life, and does not add to it.[7]

In the case of music and painting, Lewis says that one is "using" a work if one approaches it as a means of calling up memories, of reminding one of something else. We may like a certain tune because we remember where we were or who we were with when we first heard it. A Norman Rockwell painting may remind us of our grandmother or the town where we grew up. A painting thus used is like a child's teddy bear. The child isn't interested in the teddy bear as a work of art (though the parents may be). In fact too much attention to the teddy bear's aesthetic qualities will distract from its capabilities as a trigger for the imagination. Playing with the teddy bear is, and ought to be, all a matter of "pretend."

With a work of art, on the other hand, whether visual, musical, or literary, we will miss what it holds for us if we enter into our subjective "play" before allowing it to "work" on us.

We sit down before the picture in order to have something done to us, not that we may do things with it. The first demand any work of any art makes upon us is surrender. Look. Listen. Receive. Get yourself out of the way. (There is no good asking first whether the work before you deserves such a surrender, for until you have surrendered you cannot possibly find out.)[8]

Lewis does not suggest that appreciating art is entirely passive for the "receiver" of a work of art:

His is also an imaginative activity; but an obedient one. He seems passive at first because he is making sure of his orders. If, when they have been fully grasped, he decides that they are not worth obeying — in other words, that this is a bad picture — he turns away altogether.[9]

Lewis concludes from this that it is wrong to say that the majority "enjoy bad pictures." "They enjoy the ideas suggested to them by bad pictures. They do not really see the pictures as they are. If they did, they could not live with them." Although Lewis lived prior to the introduction of those velvet paintings of cutesy-wootsy wide-eyed children, one can imagine what he would have said about people who say they like them. He would say that they like what the painting suggests to them: childhood, innocence, pathos, playfulness. What they like is some experience with children that they bring to the picture and are reminded of.

GOOD FORM

Throughout Lewis's book, he develops the argument that the enjoyment of literature requires the enjoyment of something *literary*: that is, there is something in the form of the work, in the choice and sound of words, in the rhythm, color, texture, and smell of the prose, in the pacing of the entire structure, in the way the work *exists*, that grips the better reader. Those who read lesser fiction want *action*, what Aristotle called *spectacle*. If the prose was completely recast, but the story remained the same, with all of the exciting "scenes" intact, they would not mind, if indeed they noticed.

A great work of literature (or any other art) can withstand repeated, intense scrutiny. As Lewis puts it, "The ideally bad book is the one of which a good reading is impossible. The words in which it exists will not bear close attention, and what they communicate offers you nothing unless you are prepared either for mere thrills or for flattering daydreams."[10]

"Receiving" a work of literature does not involve agreeing with it. In fact, Lewis says that reading a literary work in order to extract from it a "philosophy of life" is another way of "using" it. In reading imaginative work,

> . . . we should be much less concerned with altering our own opinions [or, we might add, in reinforcing them] — though this of course is sometimes their effect — than with entering fully into the opinions, and therefore also the attitudes, feelings and total experience, of other men. Who in his ordinary senses would try to decide between the claims of materialism and theism by reading Lucretius and Dante? But who in his literary senses would not delightedly learn from them a great deal about what it is like to be a materialist or a theist?
>
> In good reading there ought to be no "problem of belief." I read Lucretius and Dante at a time when (by and large) I agreed with Lucretius. I have read them since I came (by and large) to agree with Dante. I cannot find that this has much altered my experience, or at all altered my evaluation, of either. A true lover of literature should be in one way like a honest examiner, who is prepared to give the highest marks to the telling, felicitous and well-documented exposition of views he dissents from or even abominates.[11]

Now Lewis has no doubt stepped on some Christian toes here. For many Christians insist that "good" literature must be "orthodox" literature, that anything worth reading should be the product of a Christian worldview. Before going on, we should note that such people are more likely to talk about "reading material" than "literature," which leads us to suspect that they are users rather than receivers of literature. This point is very important for our understanding of popular culture, for *if* Lewis is right, that high art is best received rather than used, and *if* popular art is always used because it is incapable of being received, then isn't popular art *per se* safer for Christians than high art? If receiving a work means we may find ourselves acknowledging its genius as literature, despite its embodying what we may judge to be a defective worldview, wouldn't it be better to remain users, and not put ourselves (and our children) in the embarrassing and potentially dangerous position of admiring the wicked and the apostate?

It might be easier (at least in the short run), but it would not be better. For if we insist on remaining users, we are effectively denying the existence of a realm of God's creation. We are saying that the aesthetic quality of a work can be reduced to its instructional, moral quality. This is no less reductionistic than saying that all of life can be reduced to political concerns.

Moreover, the aesthetic power of works by unbelieving artists is still there. If we make the mistake of assuming that the only good art is art that is theologically sound, then when we come across a work of art so powerful that its artistic worth cannot be denied, we might assume that its theology is sound. The logic runs as follows: All good art is theologically sound. This is good art. Therefore this is theologically sound.

There are Christians who behave this way. (At one time, I did so myself.) I believe this is why it is not uncommon to find artists who are professing Christians, but who have so many faulty ideas about Christian orthodoxy (if they allow the category of orthodoxy at all). It also explains why, when some Christians are moved by a work, they find it easy to assume the artist is a Christian. I once knew someone who insisted that a particular composer *must* have been a Christian because his music was so powerful.

TWO KINDS OF GOODNESS

The solution to this dilemma is to recognize that aesthetic "goodness" is not the same as moral "goodness" — that the word "good" in the phrase *good art* is not a moral evaluation. Lewis is very hard on critics he calls the "Vigilants." These are moralists and ideologues of all sorts, critics whose "conception of what is good in literature makes a seamless whole with their total conception of the good life. . . . The Vigilants . . . [find] in every turn of expression the symptom of attitudes which it is a matter of life and death to accept or resist. . . . They admit no such realm of experience as the aesthetic. There is for them no specifically literary good. . . ."[12]

Clement Greenberg made the same point in his discussion of popular culture, which, you may remember, he labeled "kitsch." He noted that kitsch erases the distinction between values in life and values in art entirely. Kitsch is attractive precisely because "there is no discontinuity between art and life, no need to accept a convention."[13] Accustomed to using pictures rather than receiving them, the devotee of popular culture says, "Sure, Norman Rockwell is a better painter than Picasso, 'cause I know a young boy who looked just like that one on the cover of the *Saturday Evening Post* when he got his first haircut, but I've *never* met a woman like those lasses in *Les Demoiselles d'Avignon.*"

Ironically, the ability to say that a work of art can be aesthetically good, but false in the worldview it assumes provides an opportunity for the cultivation of moral capacities that popular culture cannot offer. Toward the end of his book, Lewis ponders the question of why we like a work of literature that we don't agree with. He observes that one could enjoy the work of the poet A. E. Houseman and that of G. K. Chesterton, but one couldn't possibly agree with both of them on their views of life. (Chesterton was an orthodox Catholic, while Houseman, musing on creation, once wrote: "Whatever brute and blackguard made the world. . . .")

Earlier in the book, Lewis talks of reading D. H. Lawrence, whose work was obviously influenced by the philosophy of Bergson, a philosophy Lewis calls "biolatry," the worship of life. Lewis says that one could enjoy Lawrence's embodiment of such a philosophy "while clearly judging, as if with some other part of the mind, that this sort of [philosophy] and the conclusions drawn from it are very muddled and perhaps pernicious."[14]

How can one enjoy such literature? Lewis says that the best explanation he can come up with is that "we seek an enlargement of our being. . . . Each of us by nature sees the whole world from one point of view with a perspective and a selectiveness peculiar to himself. . . . We want to see with other eyes, to imagine with other imaginations, to feel with other hearts, as well as with our own."[15] This may sound like the most irresponsible escapism at first. After all, didn't God create you as you? Shouldn't you be content with your own perspective?

Lewis suggests that we think about how we transcend our

limited viewpoint in three other areas of experience: love, morality, and the pursuit of knowledge:

> In love we escape from our self into one other. In the moral sphere, every act of justice or charity involves putting ourselves in the other person's place and thus transcending our own competitive particularity. In coming to understand anything we are rejecting the facts as they are for us in favour of the facts as they are. The primary impulse of each is to maintain and aggrandise himself. The secondary impulse is to go out of the self, to correct its provincialism and heal its loneliness. In love, in virtue, in the pursuit of knowledge, and in the reception of the arts, we are doing this. Obviously this process can be described either as an enlargement or as a temporary annihilation of the self. But that is an old paradox; "he that loseth his life shall save it."[16]

In transcending our own limited perspective, says Lewis, we are more ourselves than ever.

We seem to have come rather far from popular culture. But since our purpose in this and the previous chapter was to consider how the aesthetic capacity of popular culture differed from that of high art, we have actually come to the most significant question yet raised about popular culture. If what we do when we pursue an interest in high art is in some way similar to what we do in loving someone, in showing justice and mercy, and in the pursuit of knowledge, can enjoyment of the arts (as recipients, not as users) cultivate in us certain skills that seep over into these other areas of life? Are there natural virtues of sympathy, of love, of justice, of mercy, of wisdom that can be encouraged by aesthetic experience? According to Lewis, learning to "receive" a work of art does encourage habits of the heart that have effects in other areas of life.

And now, to put popular culture on the spot, does it have the same capacities? No, and few people, even its most ardent fans, would claim that it does. Is a life influenced more by the ethos of popular culture than by that of high culture thereby deprived in some significant way? Probably. Is my answer a cop-out? Well, we're not talking about batting averages, right? I can't prove it scientifically. There is no clearcut Biblical teaching on this, although my conclusions have been developed as a response to the exhortations to get wisdom. There are some Biblical teachings which suggest that the virtues promoted by high culture (in its best, not its decadent forms) have some spiritual value that popular culture cannot achieve.

IN SEARCH OF EXCELLENCE

First, in Philippians 4:8, Paul writes, "Whatever is true, whatever is noble, whatever is right, whatever is pure, whatever is lovely, whatever is admirable — if anything is excellent or praiseworthy — think about such things." Paul is commanding the Philippian Christians (and, by extension, all believers) to discipline their minds and hearts to reflect on excellence. He does not qualify his statement to say they should only think about excellent "spiritual" matters, matters pertaining to God directly. So it seems legitimate to believe that anything in the created realm that qualifies as being excellent or praiseworthy is good to reflect upon.

Furthermore, Paul does not say that we should reflect on what we *think* is lovely, or whatever we *feel* is admirable. We are to give sustained attention to whatever is *objectively* true and noble and right. One of the greatest problems with the way popular culture works is that it is so subjective. Praiseworthiness tends to be established by the market rather than by any objective standard.

In order to recognize what is true, noble, right, pure, lovely, and admirable, we need to be able to recognize what is false, ignoble, wrong, impure, unlovely, and justly unadmired. But such categories are almost never applied to popular culture within its own borders, so to speak. In 1989 the Grammy Awards added a category for heavy metal bands. Is heavy metal noble and pure? Did any Grammy official raise such a question? Can you imagine an adolescent rock fan trying to persuade his peers that any song at the top of the charts lacks a sense of truth? One of the greatest limitations of the popular culture aesthetic is that it does not encourage the application of such objective categories.

Such subjectivist limitations are perhaps most evident when the aesthetic of popular culture has invaded the liturgy of the church. Consider this scenario. In your church next Sunday morning, a very earnest soloist sings a piece of music that is exceedingly trite, clichéd, maudlin, and pretentious. You believe that such liturgical expression misses the mark set by Philippians 4:8 considerably. While the text it presented was generally true (though tainted by sentimentality), the music was not true, noble, lovely, or admirable. If the soloist had some classical music training, you might stand a chance of persuading her that this was the case. Classical music critics all have their own taste, but at least such categories are operating in their work, and they insist on distinguishing masterworks from schlock.

But try telling someone from the Barry Manilow School of Liturgy that something is schlock and they will regard you as an arrogant elitist. *You* say the music was not true, noble, or admirable; *they* say it was a "blessing" for them. But is their "blessing" purely a subjective matter? For popular culture enthusiasts, if it feels good, it *is* good. You could never persuade your parents that Lawrence Welk's repertoire was not really very true or noble or admirable. There were no objective standards you could appeal to. It was just a matter of *taste*. One man's kitsch is another man's art. Popular culture's aesthetics can only interpret Philippians 4:8 in a subjectivist manner. That alone should make it suspect as a dominant cultural form.

The subjectivism of popular culture renders null and void any concept of propriety. In social behavior, propriety refers to actions that are appropriate or fitting to the circumstances. At root, the word refers to the true nature of things, their *properties*. Today how we behave in the presence of others is often said to be a wholly subjective matter. There *is* no true nature of things: all significance is defined by the self. Therefore, any action in any setting is justified, as long as it is "authentic."

The dominance of popular culture has certainly contributed to this social egotism. The aesthetics of popular culture define fittingness solely in terms of the self's desires and the market (which is, after all, a collection of many desiring selves), not by any objective standards.

In the example given above, the church soloist's selection raises questions of propriety. Because many Christians have adopted the subjectivism of popular culture, questions of the aesthetics of liturgical expression are usually reduced to a question of "what the market (i.e., the congregation's tastes) will bear." As a result, not only does a lot of kitsch end up in worship services, but so does a lot of good music that doesn't belong there. I remember a worship service that ended with a performance of part of the "Organ Symphony" by Camille Saint-Saëns, a big, blustery showpiece that is a wonderful occasion for an organist to show off, but totally inappropriate to close a service that featured a sermon on humility. Most of the congregation stood in rapt attention until the work was finished, then applauded appreciatively. It *was* a good performance, but it was lousy liturgy. I suspect, however, that raising the question of propriety would have puzzled many of the parishoners.

Of course, propriety is not simply a category that applies to aesthetics. Could it be that one of the causes of the decline of attention to manners, those habits of behavior that allow us to demonstrate respect and honor to those to whom it is due (a Christian duty), is the triumph of popular culture's ways?

Another text that has some relevance here is Colossians 3:1, 2. Paul writes: "Since, then, you have been raised with Christ, set your hearts on things above, where Christ is seated at the right hand of God. Set your minds on things above, not on earthly things." In this context, it is quite clear that Paul is commanding that believers not only direct their attention to good and true things, but to eternal, salvific, holy, and heavenly things. We should not become preoccupied with earthly culture of any sort, neither Bach *nor* Bon Jovi. But we cannot escape cultural influences. We will still have some ornamentation in our churches and homes. We will hang something on our walls and use some fabric to curtain our windows. We will still sing some music in church. So while we may establish the norms for our lives by setting our minds on heavenly things, we still are living with and among earthly things.

Applying Paul's command to cultural matters, it would seem that our choice of cultural influences should be governed by the first duty to transcend our earthly preoccupations. Which cultural ethos and set of experiences provide the most encouragement for reflection on the transcendent? Popular culture is extremely deficient in this regard. It emphasizes the self and the present. Its perspective is that of here and now, and *you* and your experiences are the arbiter of all things. Such a starting point would seem to be an obstacle to the duty to develop a sense of the transcendent realities of Christ at the right hand of God. If the aesthetic of popular culture has difficulty transcending the self and the immediate moment, how can it hope to inculcate a sense of an even greater transcendence?

Biblical Christianity teaches that the self is not self-defining. We are all created in the image of God, whether or not we want to be. We all stand in judgment before a holy God, whether or not we want to. We have all been given certain natural abilities, opportunities, frustrations, and liabilities by a sovereign God. We do not, as many would have us believe, "create our own reality." There is one reality, ordered by the one God. We are answerable to Him for our conduct within that reality. Our cultural life should encourage us to acknowledge that reality and its center in Jesus Christ, not in our self. At root, popular culture's dynamics tend to encourage a self-centeredness that Christians ought to avoid.

One last note: A good, healthy cultural life is not in itself a spiritual good. One can be fully devoted to that which is true, noble, right, pure, lovely, and admirable in the created order and *still* not recognize the Creator. Likewise, one can be surrounded by cultural garbage and enjoy the fruits of the Spirit in great abundance. But one's cultural life is not a matter of indifference either, any more than one's physical health is. A very sick person can be a very holy person, but generally it would be better if they weren't sick. Health gives one opportunities for Christian service, for more time spent in Bible study and prayer, for more fellowship with other Christians, for participating fully in the life of the visible church. If I get a good night's sleep, I find it easier to love my family, and they find it easier to recognize my love. To the extent that we guard our health, we add to our usefulness in the Body of Christ.

If our cultural lives are sick, it is likely to be an impediment to our spiritual lives. Much popular culture promotes a spirit of restlessness. That is likely to be an obstacle to prayer, to concerted reflection, and to attentiveness to the needs of others. Popular culture also has an extremely limited range of sensibilities. I have never heard a work of popular music that has the depth of poignancy of the opening bars of Brahms's "German Requiem," for example, with its text, "Blessed are they that mourn, for they shall be comforted." I learn something about mourning when I hear Brahms; I know of no similar lessons in popular music.[17]

To recollect Abraham Kaplan's remark, I did not know such feelings until I heard these works. Now that I know them, I think that I *know* something about grief, sorrow, and suffering that I did not know before. Reflecting on Jesus' identity as a man of sorrows acquainted with grief has more meaning for me than it did before. As human experience is deepened or broadened by aesthetic experience, human compassion and sympathy are enriched. These natural virtues are not to be identified with the fruit of the Spirit, but they *can* be an aid to spiritual obedience.

BEFORE THE REVOLUTION

THE TWENTY-YEAR DECADE

In 1948, Los Angeles County passed a new ordinance to prevent the sale of any publications depicting "the commission or attempted commission of the crimes of arson, assault with caustic chemicals, assault with a deadly weapon, burglary, kidnapping, mayhem, murder, rape, robbery, theft, or voluntary manslaughter."

It is hard to believe that the home of Hollywood would ever pass such a law, especially as late as 1948. The law was directed at a form of popular culture that was very hotly debated in the 1940s and 1950s, but which attracts very little attention today: the comic book.[1]

The idea of such a law passing today is unthinkable, not only because of the watchful presence of the guardians of civil liberties in the ACLU and in the media, but also because it is hard to imagine the cultural consensus necessary to effect such legislation. Today the vivid visual depiction of such crimes on television programs such as *America's Most Wanted* is considered a public service by most Americans and a public nuisance only by a small band of critics.

What caused such a radical change in the cultural mood? As recently as the late 1950s, popular culture was a serious "social issue" debated by philosophers, critics, and educators. By the late 1980s, you could do your Masters' thesis on "Leave it to Beaver." What happened?

What happened was The Sixties.

When people talk about The Sixties, they are not really talking about a decade, but about a revolution in culture. *The Sixties* is a phrase that happens to have a numerical form, but it is a phrase that is more like *The Reformation* or *The Enlightenment,* summarizing a range of ideas, social and cultural realignments, and changes in popular consciousness. The 1960s lasted from 1960 to 1969, but The Sixties began in about 1952 and didn't end until at least 1973.

"It was like a flying saucer landed," said Bob Dylan, looking back on that turbulent period from the vantage point of 1985. "That's what The Sixties were like. Everybody heard about it, but only a few really saw it."[2] Not only did everybody hear about it, but the lives of all Americans have been changed by it, whether or not they are aware that anything happened.

One of the things that happened in the 1960s themselves because of The Sixties was an apparently lasting change in attitudes about culture. William L. O'Neill, in his aptly titled book about the 1960s, *Coming Apart,* described it this way:

> Cultivated people used to feel that there was a clear line between high culture and popular culture. . . . In the 1960s this simple faith, already badly strained, collapsed. The resulting inability to distinguish between art and entertainment was one of the two most important cultural facts of the 1960s. The other was the growth of what became known as the counterculture. It was related to the first in that critical standards had to blur if what the counter-culture did was to be called art. And, as morality followed art, the old moral values had to give way if the new standards were to be called virtuous.[3]

In 1968 David Cross, a critic sympathetic to these changes, wrote in the journal *Radical America,* "high culture has lost its transcendent spirituality" and "has become subject to the laws of the market."[4] Art critic Hilton Kramer, who was at the *New York Times* when the flying saucer landed, has a similar analysis. In an article written after the death of Andy Warhol in 1987, Kramer attributes Warhol's success to his genius for the world of fashion. By the late-1950s, argues Kramer, the values of the fashion world had come to dominate the world of high culture. Pop Art, the movement identified in the public mind with Warhol, was simply the formal recognition of that fact. Warhol had worked in fashion illustration (shoes were his beat), but he cannily realized where the prestige and the money was: in the increasingly degraded world of art.

> Art, no matter how debased, still offered a kind of status that was denied to advertising, but otherwise there were now fewer and fewer differences separating the art world from the advertising world. The ethos was getting to be essentially the same. Success was the goal, the media would provide the means of achieving it, and what the media loved more than anything else — certainly more than art — was a product based on their own stock-in-trade. . . .
> As everyone knows, the art world never really recovered from this fateful incursion. As a movement Pop Art came and went in a flash, but it was a kind of flash that left everything changed. The art public was now a different public — larger, to be sure, but less serious, less introspective, less willing or able to distinguish between achievement and its trashy simulacrum. Moreover, everything connected with the life of art — everything, anyway, that might have been expected to offer some resistance to this wholesale vulgarization and demoralization — was now cheapened and corrupted. . . . When the boundary separating art and fashion was breached, so was the dividing line between high art and popular culture, and upon all those institutions and professions which have been painstakingly created to preserve high art from the corruptions of popular culture the effect was devastating. Some surrendered their standards with greater alacrity than others, but the drift was unmistakable and all in the same direction — and the momentum has only accelerated with the passage of time.[5]

High culture, with its disciplines, standards, and convictions about truth, about objective reality, about the dignity of man, surrendered to popular culture and adapted its ways. As long as art was dominated by the dynamics of fashion, such serious concerns were out of the question. As one observer has explained, "Of clear distinctions, of questions of good and bad, of how things really are, the fashionable mind could hardly care less. It never asks of itself, what do I truly think, what do I really believe, but instead, what can I get away with appearing to believe?"[6]

KNOBBY KNEES

But the artists, collectors, and art promoters aren't the only ones to blame for this cultural degeneration. The critics, those who have traditionally been the guardians of culture, were worse than negligent. Joseph Epstein has observed that when art critics are performing their "proper tutelary and evaluative job, art is in the position, to adopt a sports metaphor, of a confident and well-coached team." But such rigorous duties have been ignored.

> Instead of performing the function of a coach, over the past fifteen or twenty years criticism has become a cheerleader. Jumping up and down, screaming on the sidelines, displaying its knobby knees and occasionally revealing itself to be wearing no underpants under its short skirt, it has not only lost control of the game but has become an off-the-field exhibition of its own. Meanwhile, out on the field, players shuffle in and out, every man for himself, each running his own eccentric patterns, while confusion reigns and the game all but falls apart. Such is the condition of art . . . in our day.[7]

The story of how and why this chaotic state of affairs came to be reveals a great deal about the significance of the new dominance of popular culture in American society. But before we begin to examine that story, something should be noted about the place of American evangelicals in the midst of this cultural change.

At the beginning of the 1960s, evangelicals were for the most part inhabiting a cultural ghetto. They were invisible to mainstream culture, and didn't much care. They were not engaged with the cultural debates dominated by intellectual leaders of the 1950s, thinkers and writers such as Hannah Arendt, T. S. Eliot, Reinhold Niebuhr, Lionel Trilling, or Jacques Barzun.

One of the signs of the emergence of evangelicalism from its self-imposed cultural ghetto was the publication in the late 1960s of the early works of Francis Schaeffer. For the first time, issues in the arts and humanities were given attention by nonspecialists. Evangelical laymen were reading about John Cage and Jean-Paul Sartre. In 1970, InterVarsity Press published a book by an art historian from the Free University of Amsterdam, H. R. Rookmaaker, called *Modern Art and the Death of a Culture*. Evangelical Christians began paying serious attention to high culture *at the very moment when high culture was no longer serious about itself*.

For many young, culturally sensitive evangelicals, this seemed like a cruel trick. They were finally given the key to the museum, but were told that it was now an unclean place. They were given tickets to the concert hall, but were warned that the sounds they heard there would corrupt their souls.

Some evangelicals responded to the Schaeffer-Rookmaaker critiques by staying away from high culture altogether, which was never the intention of either man. Others, more interested in "celebrating creativity" than in serious reflection on culture, rejected the critiques as reactionary, and tried to embrace whatever the commercialized art world dished up. Still others, more politicized in their response, came to regard the defense of the distinction between high and popular culture as un-Christian, because it sided with the powerful and the wealthy against the powerless and the poor. Both of these latter groups saw The Sixties as essentially a good thing for American culture.

FROM ELVIS TO AMY

The vast majority of evangelicals never heard of Rookmaaker or his critique. For those growing up in the 1950s and 1960s, all they knew was that they were once told that rock 'n' roll was off-limits. But by 1970 the Byrds were singing "Jesus Is Just Alright" (they had performed "Turn! Turn! Turn!," with its text from Ecclesiastes, in 1965), and Judy Collins took "Amazing Grace" to the top twenty. Larry Norman asked, "Why Should the Devil Have All the Good Music?" B.J. Thomas extolled the "Mighty Clouds of Joy" ("Holy Jesus, let your love seize us, Jesus"). By the late 1970s, rock was well entrenched, not only as an acceptable option for listening, but as an increasingly prevalent form in church services which were once dominated by high culture or traditional culture. Amy Grant, Sandi Patti, and Scott Wesley Brown are now more likely to be setting the cultural agenda for evangelicals than are Benjamin Britten, Christopher Parkening, or John Rutter. (And if you recognize the first bunch of names but not the second, the point is confirmed.) The dominance of popular culture in the church is one way the twentieth-century church has uncritically appropriated the values of the world.

SIGNS OF THE TIMES

Since Christians believe that the human condition of rebellion against God is a constant, they are sometimes tempted to flatten out history, to present cultural movements as mere variations on a theme first enunciated in the Garden of Eden. All human activity *is* that, but it is not *only* that. "You know how to interpret the appearance of the sky," Jesus once warned "but you cannot interpret the signs of the times." He was talking there about epochs of redemptive history, but in the period between His comings there are signs and seasons as well. One of the times that posted some very significant signs was the nineteenth century, the age of Romanticism. The unquestioned dominance of popular culture in our society had its genesis in an era long before The Sixties, in garrets, studios, and cafés far away from Hollywood and New York.

Jacques Barzun has pointed out that eighteenth-century Liberalism (the cult of the self) and eighteenth-century Rationalism (the cult of reason) had the effect of making religion seem superfluous. If man is his own master, and reason his only judge, what is man to do with the lingering sense that there is more to life than his reason and the material world can contain?

When life has been stripped and sanitized by reason — or at least by discourse that sounds like reason — the unsatisfied desires that are left over must find some outlet. . . . What happened was that the thoughtful, the cultivated, the restless and disaffected made a religion of art. . . . The artist, renamed genius, became a hero; and for all those who could not recapture their lost faith in the ecclesiastical revivals of the period, the devotion to art became a passion.[8]

It is in Romanticism that we see the beginnings of what was later called the "adversary culture," the notion that intellectuals and artists had a calling to oppose whatever the dominant norms of the culture at large were. By the late nineteenth century, many artists and intellectuals believed that in their circles alone was there any virtue in the world. Barzun says that this angry, despising cultural elite became "dedicated to the cult of contempt for whatever is not art. Society, government, business, the professions, common tastes and manners, ambition, faith, morals, and indeed anything savoring of the norm are condemned with as fierce animus as ever moved nihilists to throw bombs at emperors and kings." But there was a great irony in their rebellion. For just as a Christian view of the dignity of man as created in the image of God gave rise to the heresy of Liberalism, the idea that man was *all* that mattered, so Liberalism's individualism and rationalism provided the social freedom for a movement that shook its fist in the face of Liberalism. Liberalism created the demon that would threaten to destroy it.

SWEPT AWAY

Many portents of The Sixties were evident in the Romanticism of the late nineteenth century. Roger Shattuck cites four traits that characterized the era: the cult of childhood, which attacked education and society at large for introducing concern about self-control; the delight in humor, especially in the absurd; the confusion between reality and fantasy; and a preference for ambiguity over clarity.[9] Shattuck says that these four qualities "manifest an unrelenting desire to dredge up new material from within, from the subconscious." The pursuit of this inner "truth" by the Romantics was encouraged by two factors: "uninhibited subjectivity and interest in occult knowledge."[10]

In his study of the "disastrous history" of Romanticism, *Deliberate Regression*, Robert Harbison says that the movement began in the "despair at a world without God," and continued because of man's "continuing need for transcendence after the supernatural is gone. The furthest excess of Romantic individualism is to recreate a god in the self out of just those parts beyond one's conscious control, so the unconscious and ungovernable is elevated as the true beyond."[11] The new god of the artist was omnipotent and self-sufficient. In his power lay the capabilities of recreating the world in his own image.

By the late nineteenth century, Romanticism had begotten Modernism. The family likeness was evident, but the son was destined to use all the tricks he had learned from the father to slay him.

It is difficult to appreciate how new Modernism in the arts was felt to be when it first burst on the scene in the late nineteenth century. Art historian Herbert Read, writing in 1933, pointed out that every generation sees a significant change in artistic styles, and about once a century there has been a "wider or deeper change of sensibility which is recognized as a period," such as the Baroque, the Classical, or the Romantic eras. But Modernism was "not so much a revolution, which implies a turning over, even a turning back, but rather a break-up, a devolution, some would say a dissolution. Its character is catastrophic. . . . The aim of five centuries of European effort is openly abandoned."[12]

In his inaugural lecture at Cambridge in 1954, C. S. Lewis expressed a similar sense that Modernism marked a decisive break with the past. He maintained that it was the greatest division in the entire history of Western man, greater than the difference between Antiquity and the Dark Ages, greater than that between the Dark and the Middle Ages, greater even than that between the Middle Ages and the Renaissance.

One of the factors that rendered the chasm between Modernism and earlier ages so deep was the "un-christening of

Europe" — that is, the lapsing of Western civilization from a Christian ethos to a post-Christian one. This, Lewis argued, was a more traumatic cultural change than the "christening" of Europe during the time of Constantine, because "Christians and Pagans had much more in common with each other than either has with a post-Christian. The gap between those who worship different gods is not so wide as that between those who worship and those who do not."[13] Some Christians might balk at this, arguing that everybody worships *something*. But not everyone worships something *consciously*. Lewis is concerned not with *spiritual* but with *cultural* change.

A society in which visible and influential religious belief and practice are the norm is culturally very much different from one in which they are the exception. Lewis warned his audience not to equate *post-Christian* culture with *pagan* culture. "A post-Christian man is not a Pagan; you might as well think that a married woman recovers her virginity by divorce. The post-Christian is separated from the Christian past and therefore doubly from the Pagan past."[14] The post-Christian is not only cut off from the theistic world of Dante, but from the polytheistic world of Virgil.

As to the effect of the radical transformation of Modernism on high culture, Lewis was quite clear, especially concerning its effect on poetry:

> I do not think that any previous age produced work which was, in its own time, as shatteringly and bewilderingly new as that of the Cubists, the Dadaists, the Surrealists, and Picasso has been in ours. And I am quite sure this is true . . . of poetry. . . . I do not see how anyone can doubt that modern poetry is not only a greater novelty than any other "new poetry" but new in a new way, almost in a new dimension.[15]

It was, as has been noted, the dislocating effects of modernity that called Modernism into being. While the Romantics had paved the way, they could never have foreseen the social and cultural metamorphosis that was to occur during the lifetime of the generation that came to maturity at the turn of the century. The earth was in many ways a completely different planet. Modernism was the necessary cultural response to the sense of being strangers in a strange land. Malcolm Bradbury and James McFarlane have summarized this diagnosis of Modernism:

> It is the one art that responds to the scenario of our chaos. It is the art consequent on Heisenberg's "Uncertainty Principle," of the destruction of civilization in the First World War, of the world changed and reinterpreted by Marx, Freud and Darwin, of capitalism and constant industrial acceleration, of existential exposure to meaninglessness or absurdity. It is the literature of technology. It is the art consequent on the dis-establishing of communal reality and conventional notions of causality, on the destruction of traditional notions of the wholeness of the individual character, on the linguistic chaos that ensues when public notions of language have been discredited and when all realities have become subjective fictions. Modernism is then the art of modernization.[16]

There is no question that Modernism produced a great wave of creativity. But, as Daniel Bell has remarked, the cost was extremely high, including "the loss of coherence in culture, particularly in the spread of an antinomian attitude to moral norms and even to the idea of cultural judgment itself."[17] The proponents of Modernism were fully self-conscious that they were riding on a wave of destruction. In 1905, impresario Sergei Diaghilev of the innovative Ballets Russe proposed an enthusiastic and fatalistic toast:

> We are witnesses of the greatest moment of summing-up in history, in the name of a new and unknown culture, which will be created by us, and which will also sweep us away. That is why, without fear or misgiving, I raise my glass to the ruined walls of the beautiful palaces, as well as to the new commandments of a new aesthetic. The only wish that I, an incorrigible sensualist, can express, is that the forthcoming struggle should not damage the amenities of life, and that the death should be as beautiful and as illuminating as the resurrection.[18]

The same year, one of the first schools of truly modern art had its first major exhibition in Paris. Called Les Fauves ("wild beasts"), these painters (including Henri Matisse, André Derain, and Maurice Vlaminck) worked in a style characterized by an unprecedented freedom of expression. Vlaminck, looking back years later, reflected:

My enthusiasm allowed me to take all sorts of liberties. I did not want to follow a conventional way of painting; I wanted to revolutionize habits and contemporary life — to liberate nature, to free it from the authority of old theories and classicism, which I hated as much as I had hated the general or the colonel of my regiment. I was filled neither with jealousy or hate, but I felt a tremendous urge to re-create a new world seen through my own eyes, a world which was entirely mine.[19]

Vlaminck's association of hatred for military authority and the rigors of high culture have an interesting resonance with The Sixties. And his urge to recreate a new world that was entirely his own is reminiscent of an American Romantic poet of an earlier generation whose work would be read by many of the prophets of The Sixties, including Allen Ginsberg. In "Song of Myself," part of *Leaves of Grass*, Walt Whitman had written:

I celebrate myself, and sing myself,
    And what I assume you shall assume,
For every atom belonging to me
    As good belongs to you.

The hatred that Vlaminck both acknowledged and denied was characteristic of Modernism. Jacques Barzun referred above to the cult of contempt that originated with the Romantics. Daniel Bell says that a *rage against order* is one of the characteristic themes of Modernism. For the Modernist, "the crucial insistence is that experience is to have no boundaries to its cravings, that there be 'nothing sacred.'"[20] Of course, one must ask if such rage isn't justified. If there is no God, no source of order, how dare society impose an arbitrary order on my life?

Another significant attribute of Modernism, which would blossom in The Sixties and which characterizes the dominance of popular culture, is what Bell calls "the eclipse of distance." This is what popular culture promises in offering everything to us immediately. Popular culture says, in effect, that nothing worthwhile is beyond your reach right now. Any experience, sensation, idea, or fantasy can be yours if you have enough money (which easy credit can guarantee), confidence (which an underarm spray can make you Sure of), and sex appeal (the product of the right toothpaste). You need not wait for greater maturity, insight, wisdom, or perceptiveness. There is no distance between you and any good thing.

Modernism's project, cheaply consummated in popular culture, was, as Daniel Bell explains, "the effort to achieve immediacy, impact, simultaneity, and sensation by eliminating aesthetic and psychic distance." In so doing, "one annihilates contemplation and envelops the spectator in the experience."[21] One also exalts instinct and impulse over reason and will.

THE MEDIUM IS THE MESSAGE

A third characteristic that Bell sees in Modernism is a "preoccupation with the medium." The medium of art, the texture of the paint, the sound of breathing or "prepared pianos" in music, the abstract properties of language in poetry and prose: all of these are of much more significance to the modernist artist than content or even form. The reason for this is rather complex, and deserves some attention. Clement Greenberg, in his essay "Avant-Garde and Kitsch," observed that modernity has made it difficult to assume anything about anything. "All the verities involved by religion, authority, tradition, style, are thrown into question, and the writer or artist is no longer able to estimate the response of his audience to the symbols and references with which he works."[22] Renoir once said that painting done for a community was possible when painters and community shared the same vision of the world and the same faith. Critic Suzi Gablik muses on the effects on artists of the loss of a shared worldview and faith:

Until the modern period, art and artists had always been imbued with a quasi-religious as well as a moral and social mission, and art was very much integrated with the social and spiritual orders. One of the deepest distinctions between other historical periods and our own is that whereas in the past, belief and hope permeated all human activity — and art had a clear consensus behind it — our own epoch is characterized by disbelief and doubt. Ideas that were once quite clear and satisfactory have become vague or irrelevant.[23]

Once a painter could could paint a Crucifixion and assume that most of his audience would have a certain belief and a certain collection of emotions about the subject matter. Against the backdrop of that consensus, the painter could paint.

But now that simple state of affairs is unavailable. Not only is there no consensus on the *significance* of the Crucifixion, there is an increasing ignorance about the simplest level of *definition* of it. It would not be surprising to find a sizeable proportion of the population of the "de-christened" West who would have no idea why a man would be depicted dying on a cross. If this were just a matter of what E. D. Hirsch, Jr., calls cultural illiteracy, we might be able to remedy the situation. The problem is deeper, however, for there is no consensus about *anything*.

A painter cannot strive to be realistic if his public cannot agree on what is real. Clement Greenberg said that the rise of the avant-garde can be seen as a response to this uncertainty. Abstract and nonobjective painting, poetry, fiction, and other arts are all attempts by the artists "in effect to imitate God by creating something valid solely on its own terms."[24]Greenberg said that the artist thus turns his attention away from common experience (a building, a face, a vase of flowers) and "turns it in upon the medium of his own craft." His paintings are about painting.

But abstract, nonrepresentational art, argued Greenberg, "if it is to have aesthetic validity, cannot be arbitrary and accidental, but must stem from obedience to some worthy constraint or original." In other words, abstraction must still be true to something. Representational art strives to be true to the created order it represents. Abstract art (or music or poetry) strives to be true to the principles and disciplines of the art itself. So the subject matter of abstract art is not some created reality, but the *tradition* of depicting created reality. Greenberg borrowed Aristotle's idea of art imitating nature, and says that in abstract art we have "the imitation of imitating."[25]

Greenberg went so far as to say that this method of the avant-garde is now the only way serious art can be done: "By no other means is it possible today to create art and literature of a high order."[26] The reason for this necessity is the lack of any cultural consensus about reality. Greenberg's rigorous, demanding aesthetic, fulfilled most thoroughly in painting by the school called Abstract Expressionism, was in a sense the last gasp of high culture.

Romanticism and early Modernism had questioned all truth, and opened the door for all sorts of charlatans to pose as artistic geniuses. The avant-garde soon found itself in two opposing camps. One was progressive and radical. It asked, "If the self is the center of the universe, who is to say that one self is more centered than another?" As Hilton Kramer put it, the radical avant-garde "cancels all debts to the past in the pursuit of a new vision, however limited and fragmentary and circumscribed, and thus feels at liberty — in fact compelled — to sweep [away] anything and everything in the path of its own immediate goals, whatever the consequences."[27]

Greenberg represented the avant-garde's other wing, what Kramer called the "champions of tradition and harmony." Greenberg said, in effect, that if we have no objective reality in the created order, at least we have the reality of paint and how it has been applied through the years. We have the reality of colors and how they have been juxtaposed in the history of painting. In short, we have the tradition of art. We must be true to that, if nothing else. A similar position is represented by T. S. Eliot, one of the preeminent literary modernists, in his 1919 essay, "Tradition and the Individual Talent."

The mandate for abstraction that the Abstract Expressionists followed, and that Clement Greenberg expected all artists to follow, could not survive for long. It tied artists to an objective reality (the tradition of art), but it was a man-made reality, at least once removed from creation. Art always had the power to be true to and to elevate human experience as long as it was rooted in the real things of creation. It is in real things (fruit and trees and stars and seeds and bread and wine and water) that God's order in creation is most irresistibly, unavoidably present.

Before the Fall, God did *not* warn Adam and Eve to avoid thinking certain thoughts, to refrain from indulging in certain *abstract* behavior. He gave them a *concrete* prohibition. He established concrete modes of obedience. See that tree? Don't eat its fruit. Of course, the evil of sin does not reside in the fruit, but in using the fruit in a way God has prohibited. It is in the will, not in matter, that sin resides. But it is God's prohibition concerning the body's use of things (as directed by the will) that focuses our attention and instructs us in the perception of the more subtle sins that reside only in the heart.

Throughout the history of redemption, man has been held culpable for his relation to things. God has mediated His love and His wrath through the stuff of creation. Abram was told to cut his flesh as a seal of God's promise. Moses encountered a burning bush, struck rocks with a rod, and gathered manna fallen from Heaven. Jesus took on a human body, the noblest thing in creation, which was finally killed to fulfill God's promise. He commanded His disciples to eat bread and drink wine, a meal that signifies the restoration of what had been lost in that evil eating in the Garden. After His resurrection, He assumed a new body, a new kind of imperishable thing, capable of being touched, capable of eating in anticipation of a great marriage feast. And through His apostles, He promised His disciples a continued existence in the resurrection of *their* new bodies.

Once art abandoned the objective, demanding reality of things, and retreated into the domain of forms, no matter how disciplined and orderly the artist worked, he lost touch with God's order in creation, which was always the common factor, the link between art and human experience. The rigor required by such aesthetic discipline was really pointless if one didn't *care* about the artistic tradition. Should one care about the tradition, as George Leigh Mallory cared about Mt. Everest simply because it was *there*?

The more the nihilistic strains of Modernism took over, and the more the influence of Christianity waned in the culture and the influence of Zen Buddhism and other Eastern religions were strengthened, the harder it became for the champions of tradition and harmony to keep up the charade. The stage had been already been set for their defeat. It merely remained for the key players to assume their places. At a certain point, the adversary culture would inevitably turn around to attempt to destroy the Godless culture that had made it possible. Hell had been waiting in the wings for over a century; it finally broke loose in the 1960s.

WHERE HAVE ALL THE STANDARDS GONE?

A BRIEF INTERMISSION

It would be easy simply to assemble a collection of the outrageous and the bizarre from The Sixties and present it with little more than a moralistic "Tsk, tsk." But our purpose is not simply to confirm what we already suspect (that people who don't believe in God will believe in anything). We are looking for specific evidence of the failure of high culture, for high culture's willing embrace of the characteristics of popular culture, and the subsequent dominance of American cultural life by the dynamics of popular culture.

Before taking our whirlwind tour of The Sixties, it may be helpful to review the distinctions established so far between the characteristics and values of popular culture and those of traditional and high culture. The following list, if taken in isolation, is a bit simplistic, but it does summarize some of the general differences between the cultures.

This is admittedly a very stacked deck. It is deliberately overstated, a caricature. But caricatures can sometimes reveal a great deal about character. Also, remember that the list is intended to describe the *tendencies* of the competing cultural forms, both in their intrinsic qualities, and in the way they work when they are culturally dominant. It is no secret that I believe the

POPULAR CULTURE	TRADITIONAL AND HIGH CULTURE
Focuses on the new	Focuses on the timeless
Discourages reflection	Encourages reflection
Pursued casually to "kill time"	Pursued with deliberation
Gives us what we want, tells us what we already know	Offers us what we could not have imagined
Relies on instant accessibility; encourages impatience	Requires training; encourages patience
Emphasizes information and trivia	Emphasizes knowledge and wisdom
Encourages quantitative concerns	Encourages qualitative concerns
Celebrates fame	Celebrates ability
Appeals to sentimentality	Appeals to appropriate, pro-portioned emotions
Content and form governed by requirements of the market	Content and form governed by requirements of created order
Formulas are the substance	Formulas are the tools
Relies on spectacle, tending to violence and prurience	Relies on formal dynamics and the power of symbols (including language)
Aesthetic power in reminding of something else	Aesthetic power in intrinsic attributes
Individualistic	Communal
Leaves us where it found us	Transforms sensibilities
Incapable of deep or sustained attention	Capable of repeated, careful attention
Lacks ambiguity	Allusive, suggests the transcendent
No discontinuity between life and art	Relies on "Secondary World" conventions
Reflects the desires of the self	Encourages understanding of others
Tends toward relativism	Tends toward submission to standards
Used	Received

attributes in the second column to be more likely to encourage a healthy Christian participation in a common culture, as well as a more humane cultural existence for unbelievers.

Asserting that traditional or high culture has a greater potential for establishing a sensibility that is beneficial and constructive is not to say that all aspects of traditional or high culture are superior to all aspects of popular culture. Nor is it to say that there is some inherent virtue in being a dilettante or high cultural groupie. Such fashion-minded status seekers go to concerts and museums as a social act, much as they eat at the right restaurants and send their children to the right schools. Such hypocrisy may serve to support worthy cultural institutions, but it does little to cultivate a sensibility that enjoys the richness of cultural expressions. It is simply another way of using rather than receiving art.

Similarly, there are those whom C. S. Lewis calls "devotees of culture." These are people who visit galleries and concert halls and read all the prescribed books in the interest of self-improvement. Lewis says that such worthy and sincere activity may be as far from the real love of art "as a man who does exercises with dumb-bells every morning may be from being a lover of games."[1]

Continuing with that analogy, Lewis makes a very helpful distinction. He notes that one can enjoy playing soccer, or one can play it purely in the interests of health. Those are two very different reasons for playing, and they will probably result in two very different levels of attachment and involvement to the game. But Lewis considers a third possibility:

No doubt, a man who has a taste for games (and for overeating as well) may very properly act on the medical motive when he makes for himself a rule to give general priority to his taste for games. In the same way, a man who has a gust both for good literature and for mere time-killing with trash may reasonably, on cultural grounds, on principle, give a priority to the former. But in both instances we are presupposing a genuine gust. The first man chooses football rather than a gargantuan lunch because the game, as well as the lunch, is one of the things he enjoys. The second turns to Racine instead of E. R. Burroughs because *Andromaque*, as well as *Tarzan*, is really attractive to him. But to come to the particular game with nothing but a hygenic motive or to the tragedy with nothing but a desire for self-improvement, is not really to play the one or to receive the other. Both attitudes fix the ultimate intention on oneself.[2]

Our principal concern is with the sensibilities encouraged by popular culture versus those encouraged by high culture (as well as traditional culture). We aren't prescribing a list of preferred cultural experiences for the sake of some crusade of cultural literacy. It is important to remember that the advantage of high culture's sensibility consists in its ability to provide some transcendent perspective, while popular culture's liability consists in its tendency to encourage a self-centered perspective. Keep this in mind in the coming pages, since "high culture" isn't what it used to be. Today's high culture is not anywhere near high enough, for reasons spelled out in this and the previous chapter. In many of its forms, it is no longer interested in or capable of sustaining any connections to transcendence. So when the term "high culture" is used from here on, it is used in its historic, "ideal sense."

We now join our narrative concerning the 1960s, already in progress. But as we do, keep in mind the left-hand column above. It should soon become evident that Modernism shoved high culture onto popular culture's turf.

EVE OF DESTRUCTION

If the decade that saw the collapse of high culture into the world of entertainment required a ribbon-cutting ceremony, there could have been no better place to stage it than in New York City, that monument to modernity, friend to vaudeville and the avant-garde. On Saint Patrick's Day, 1960, a ceremony that could be regarded as a portent of the times was held in the sculpture garden of the Museum of Modern Art. Governor Nelson Rockefeller was there, as were TV crews from the three networks. It was a damp, March evening, and after nightfall the slush in the streets made it seem colder by the minute.

A celebrated European artist was hard at work as the distinguished guests assembled and the camera crews tested their equipment. The artist was Jean Tinguely, a Swiss "kinetic sculptor." He was making final adjustments on a complex work that was twenty-three feet long and twenty-seven feet high. Its dimensions are important to keep in mind, not simply to give some sense of scale, but because they are probably the only thing about the work that is comprehensible. As art critic Calvin Tomkins points out, this *magnum opus* was "a huge construction whose sole purpose is to destroy itself in one glorious act of mechanical suicide." How fitting.

> The piece is composed of scrap metal, bicycle parts, a washing machine drum, an upright piano, a radio, several electric fans, an old Addressograph, a baby's bassinet, three dozen bicycle and baby carriage wheels, uncounted small motors and fan belts, two Tinguely "meta-matics" (motor-driven devices that produce instant abstract paintings by the yard), several bottles of chemical stinks, an apparatus to make smoke, bells and Klaxons and other noisemakers, and yards and yards of metal tubing, the entire apparatus painted white and topped by an inflated orange meteorological balloon. It is called *Hommage à New-York*.

How thoughtful. One wonders if Governor Rockefeller and the good burghers of New York felt honored by this display. And it *was* twenty-three feet long and twenty-seven feet high. At about 7:30, as Tomkins put it, "the construction ends and the destruction begins."

> The great white machine rattles and shivers in all its members. Smoke pours from its interior, temporarily blanketing the audience. The piano catches fire and burns, accompanying its own demise with three mournful notes repeated over and over. Parts of the structure break loose and scuttle off to die elsewhere. Crossbeams sag as electric charges melt the

previously weakened joints. . . . One of the meta-matics tries but fails to produce a black-and-white abstract picture on a long roll of paper. The other unreels a streamer proclaiming "Yang Is Ying." A fireman, summoned by Tinguely, comes to extinguish the blaze in the piano; he is angrily booed by the spectators. After about twenty minutes it becomes clear that the machine will not perish unaided; firemen's axes finish the job, and *Hommage à New-York* returns to the junk piles from which it was born. The nineteen sixties have begun.[3]

In The Sixties, the cultural violence that had been latent in Romanticism and in its puckish progeny, Modernism, erupted into real violence in art and in life. Art, like many people coming of age, was to be found "in the streets." Daniel Bell has argued that the mood of The Sixties was essentially a concentrated form of the mood of Modernism, with some even more extreme elements thrown in for bad measure: "a concern with violence and cruelty; a preoccupation with the sexually perverse; a desire to make noise; an anticognitive and anti-intellectual mood; an effort once and for all to erase the boundary between 'art' and 'life'; and a fusion of art and politics."[4]

The 1950s have gotten a rather bad rap. They are portrayed as a period of mindless conformity. In high culture, however, the 1950s were characterized by an emphasis not on conformity, but on (in Bell's terms) "complexity, irony, ambiguity, and paradox." Such aesthetic values are not for the timid or for the undisciplined. They are not the habits of being that lend themselves to any form of sloganeering, whether it be "Off the Pigs" or "Do Your Own Thing." The aesthetic values that dominated the artistic and literary establishment in the 1950s fostered, as Bell explains, "a critical attitude, a detachment and distance which guard one against any overwhelming involvement, absorption, immolation in a creed or an experience. . . . The sensibility of the 1960s rejected that mood in savage, even mindless fashion. In its fury with the times, the new sensibility was loud, imprecatory, prone to obscenity."[5]

This fury led to the perverse notion that, in the phrase of novelist John Gardner, "the cruellest, ugliest thing we can say is likely to be the truest."[6] Gardner went on to argue that real art never believed such nonsense for a moment, but the 1960s was not a great decade for real art.

It was, instead, a decade for angry posturing, for declamation and manifestos. What is most surprising about The Sixties in retrospect is how seriously its pretensions were taken by relatively intelligent people. A sense of guilt about racism, about Vietnam, about materialism certainly contributed to the gullibility with which "The Establishment" generally accepted the criticism of some very noisy brats.

But there was also a deeper sense of inadequacy and failure that caused many adults to muse, "Who are we to criticize our idealistic youth?" As Jacques Barzun observed in 1967, "The bourgeois themselves feel and acknowledge that they are no good." They had been told that since the beginnings of Romanticism. He suggested that the virulence of the political and cultural movements of the 1960s was in part due to the premature capitulation of "the enemy." The Movement turned violent, not because it met resistance, but because it didn't meet enough. There were no absolute standards by which this children's crusade could be judged. Liberalism, with its new and overarching commandment, "Thou shalt not prefer one thing to another," had seen to that. If one's elders are willing to be "permissive" and "flexible" about one's every excess, it soon becomes clear "that there is nothing to push against but the empty air, a feeling which is at first agreeable, then is disconcerting, and ends by causing the anguish of pointlessness — the horror of the absurd."[7]

BACK TO "NO FUTURE"

But the absurd does not always seem horrible. As Samuel Beckett has demonstrated, as much of popular comedy since the 1960s has made clear, the absurd can be very funny — at least for a while. The belief that there is no hope for the future can actually eliminate a lot of anxiety if one gets to the point where the future is entirely unreal. That is the point the pioneer of nihilism, Friedrich Nietzsche, finally discovered. In 1888 he wrote a letter to a friend in which he said "that one of life's most basic concepts has been blotted out of my consciousness: that of the 'future.'" As critic Rolf-Dieter Herrmann has commented:

> Nietzsche can no longer believe in the future nor any progress in it, in this or any other life; and this is because God is dead, because there is no God nor general metaphysical principle that will justify the concept of the world as having an aim, purpose, or meaning beyond and outside itself. It is only we who are there and able to disclose the world in which we live in each moment, in the present. This emphasis upon the present has the important effect of destroying every hope beyond it. There is only the present, and something removed from us, something that we cannot approach in terms of ideas but only experience.[8]

If the present is all you have, if you can get to the point where the future has no weight in your consciousness, then there is nothing to worry about, and every experience in every moment is self-justifying. And if you can also dispense with the past, you are even less burdened. In 1967, the director of the newly opened Chicago Museum of Contemporary Art claimed that he was "not concerned with art that has already proved its point" — that is, with *any* art from the past. This is a far cry from the experience of the conservative Modernists such as Eliot and Stravinsky, who were, in Hilton Kramer's term, "tradition-haunted artists . . . mindful, above all, of the continuity of culture and thus committed to the creative renewal of its deepest impulses."[9] Small wonder that the exhibit on display at the opening of his museum was "an exhibition of artists who proclaim the end of art and demand the elimination of museums."[10] One would think their timing left something to be desired.

This future- and past-denying, present-celebrating side of nihilism is what ended up informing much of the spirit of The Sixties *and beyond*. The *Zeitgeist* of The Sixties is one in which the future has no power to intimidate and the past has no power to inspire. This emphasis on the eternal *now*, which is so characteristic of popular culture, became more and more evident in high art. It was already implicit in the late 1950s in the work of painters such as Jackson Pollock, Willem de Kooning, and Franz Kline, for whom the action of creating a painting was all that was important. As critic Harold Rosenberg put it:

> The canvas began to appear to one American painter after another as an arena in which to act — rather than as a space in which to reproduce, re-design, or "express" an object, actual or imagined. What was to go on the canvas was not a picture but an event. . . . What matters always is the revelation contained in the act.[11]

The resulting thing on the canvas was mere residue, a byproduct. Painter Robert Rauschenberg once described his work as "the leftover of some activity. The activity is the thing I'm most interested in."[12] Of course, he was not above accepting thousands of dollars from a collector who wanted to buy his leftovers.

One of Rauschenberg's associates, the composer John Cage, had a similar aesthetic, one that emphasized that his music had to do only with the present, with the moment in which it was being performed. When asked in an interview about works he had written earlier, he responded rather brusquely, "You wouldn't ask me in the case of the steak which I ate ten years ago somehow to regurgitate it and eat it over again, would you?"[13]

This emphasis on immediacy, on the experience of the moment, was evident in other arts as well. Theater, for example, began to stress improvisation and the relative insignificance of the text. Judith Malina, the director of the much celebrated Living Theatre, once said, "I don't want to be Antigone [onstage], I am and want to be Judith Malina." This "I Gotta Be Me" aesthetic is worthy of a Charles Bronson or a Clint Eastwood, since, after all, moviegoers are paying to see Charles Bronson be Charles Bronson. Let Clint be Clint. But this was rather surprising in the theater, since theater has traditionally offered something more than celebrities. Malina's insistence on playing herself involves, as Daniel Bell has observed, the denial of "the commonality of human experience. . . . To eliminate

Antigone, or deny her corporeality, is to repudiate memory and to discard the past."[14]

In literature, meanwhile, writers of the 1960s, influenced by "beat" figures such as Allen Ginsberg and Jack Kerouac, were rejecting the necessity of reflection and revision, the careful honing of thought, and were rather writing stream of consciousness works, works with a quality in some ways more like television than serious prose.

Many of the attributes of popular culture are evident in the movements in "high" art already described. But no Sixties movement served to blur the distintinction between the two sensibilities more thoroughly, in the mind of the general public and of the artists and critics, than Pop Art.

HOLY RELATIVISM, BATMAN!

The English critic Lawrence Alloway is usually credited with having coined the term *Pop Art*. He was certainly present at the birth of the movement. It was actually two movements, centered in London and in New York, springing up independently of one another, responding to the spirit of the age.

Alloway and a number of other young artists, architects, and photographers used to meet at the Institute of Contemporary Art in London to talk about their work. In the mid-1950s, they began to spend a lot of time talking about popular culture.

> We discovered that we had in common a vernacular culture that persisted beyond any special interest or skills in art, architecture, design, or art criticism that any of us might possess. The area of contact was mass-produced urban culture: movies, advertising, science fiction, Pop music. We felt none of the dislike of commercial culture standard among most intellectuals, but accepted it as a fact, discussed it in detail, and consumed it enthusiastically. One result of our discussions was to take Pop culture out of the realm of 'escapism,' 'sheer entertainment,' 'relaxation,' and to treat it with the seriousness of art.[15]

Alloway writes that he and his colleagues began to develop an "aesthetic of expendibility," a notion that art was produced to be used (and used up) and disposed of at will. Nothing lasting or permanent need be present in art. It could easily be made for the moment. It is notable that Alloway and his friends worked from a very relativistic position from the start, adopting what he called an "anthropological definition of culture, in which all types of human activity were the object of aesthetic judgement and attention."[16] In other words, anything and everything was art, if you wanted to interpret it that way.

Of course, just about everything has aesthetic qualities. But it is clear that the early British Pop artists were interested in erasing distinctions between art and everything else, so standards could not be imposed. Roy Lichtenstein, one of the most famous American Pop artists, clearly agreed with this relativism: "Pop Art looks out into the world; it appears to accept its environment, which is not good or bad, but different, another state of mind."[17]

One of the most famous early English Pop Artists was Richard Hamilton, who, in something of a manifesto, declared in rather truncated style what Pop Art should be:

Popular (designed for a mass audience)
Transient (short-term solution)
Expendable (easily forgotten)
Low-cost
Mass-produced
Young (aimed at youth)
Witty
Sexy
Gimmicky
Glamorous
Big Business. . . .[18]

But how is this aesthetic fundamentally different from MTV? How might a work produced according to these "standards" be received in the sense that C. S. Lewis prescribes? What capabilities does such art have for offering any sense of the transcendent? These are all very silly questions. They presuppose artistic goals that none of the Pop people had in view, nor did many other artists of The Sixties. Hamilton, Alloway, and all their American cousins would have agreed that there is no difference between the Pop aesthetic and that of popular culture.

The American version of Pop Art was even more casual about its relations with popular culture. "Hard-core Pop Art," wrote critic Lucy Lippard, one of the movement's big fans, "is essentially a product of America's long-finned, big-breasted, one-born-every-minute society, its advantages of being more involved with the future than the past. . . . Pop Art is instantly to the point."[19]

> Pop chose to depict everything previously considered unworthy of notice, let alone of art: every level of advertising, magazine and newspaper illustration, Times Square jokes, tasteless bric-à-brac and gaudy furnishings, ordinary clothes and foods, film stars, pin-ups, cartoons. Nothing was sacred, and the cheaper and more despicable the better.[20]

Pop Art and its superstars delighted, not in the best and the most beautiful, but in the trashiest. Art historian Dore Ashton says that Claes Oldenburg, who lived in New York's Lower East Side, "revelled in its seamy disorder, its seething street life and even its sad domain of human shipwrecks, the Bowery."[21] Far from producing work that would elevate or transcend, Pop artists were quite content to leave their viewers where they found them.

Robert Hughes has a chapter called "Culture as Nature" in his book on modern art, *The Shock of the New*. The title of the chapter suggests its theme. Once artists imitated *nature*. Today, no longer recognizing nature as the work of a Creator, they imitate *culture*. Besides, given the pursuit of novelty and the restless eagerness to pack art with pure energy, nature is boring by comparison with the culture of big, noisy machines. The culture which artists began imitating in the 1960s was popular culture: the culture of industrialized mass production and the mass media that were the mediators of machine-culture to people.

Pop Art was fascinated with the artifacts of mass production (cars, fast food, beer cans), but was even more obsessed with images and styles of the *media*: advertising and packaging (Warhol's Campbell soup cans), the cult of celebrity made possible by television (his Marilyn and Jackie silk screens), and the comics (Lichtenstein).

Robert Hughes says that the effect of Pop Art on what remained of high culture was devastating. It sold off art's "claim to seriousness" by endorsing the slogan that "the medium was the message." "All that slogan came down to," says Hughes, "was the idea that it no longer mattered what art said."22

That is a grave idea, given the history of Modernism. Art is a splendid activity, but a lousy religion. Since the Enlightenment, it was the only thing approaching a religion for many "enlightened" souls. It was the only thing that argued for the idea that being human was somehow a very significant thing. As long as art testified to something beyond the moment and beyond the material, the cultural catastrophe Nietzsche sensed in the wake of God's death could be postponed.

THEY DON'T MAKE 'EM LIKE THEY USED TO

The exhaustion of high culture meant that popular culture would fill in the void and assume the role of defining cultural styles and consciousness; traditional culture obviously couldn't step in, since the pluralism introduced by modernity made its hold on society extremely weak. But it also meant that popular culture itself would be deprived of the host on which it had parasitically existed for all of its life. The best movies, songs, musicals, and popular fiction of the period through the 1950s were created by people who were, like the early Modernists, haunted by tradition. The lyrics of a Cole Porter, the sense of drama of an Orson Welles, the rhetorical sensibility of an Edward R. Murrow were all sustained by the lingering presence of the tradition of high culture. Reminded of that tradition by such institutions as universities and museums, the proponents of popular culture paid certain, if modest, homage to the past.

When that past became largely unavailable, either through neglect or scorn, popular culture turned to itself and its own history for raw material and for sensibility. So, for example, more and more young movie directors find their imaginations fueled by (and circumscribed by) their youthful experiences with films and television. George Lucas and Steven Spielberg recall wistfully the Saturday morning serials. But the producers of those serials had probably been inspired by myths, legends, and stories of adventure preserved by folk and high culture. *Star Wars* and Indiana Jones films are more spectacular, but do they have as much of a sense of adventure as the earlier work? And what will happen to the next generation, who will look to Lucas and Spielberg as aesthetic mentors? They will be one step further removed from the rich tradition that ties them to the past. They are also more likely to be preoccupied with the technique of their craft and with special effects than with what such tales illuminate about human experience.

As popular culture becomes more and more cut off from high culture, it relies more and more on topical subject matter, rather than with lasting themes about eternal realities. Television and film producers find it easier to do a script on the social problem of the homeless than a drama about every person's need for a sense of place. AIDS is treated as an occasion to pontificate about rights and the amorality of homosexuality. The questions that terminal diseases and plagues could raise about mortality, judgment, and the quest for meaning in life are obscured, although one could easily find such themes in drama and literature of the past.

The eclipse of high culture by popular culture means, for our society, a loss of cultural memory, a loss of commitment to the future and to the past. The social effects of this are uncertain, but it is already evident that it has exacerbated a sense of desperate struggle for power within society, and has discouraged further any notion of the common good. It has also rendered the claims of Christianity more incredible than ever. The aesthetic of immediate and constant entertainment does not prepare the human consciousness well for recognition of a holy, transcendent, omnipotent, and eternal God, or to responding to His demands of repentance and obedience. It could well be that modern times will prove to be the darkest age of all.

POPULAR CULTURE'S IDIOM: ROCK AROUND THE CLOCK

ELVIS 'N' ANDY

While the artists of Pop Art were busy tearing down the walls between high culture and popular culture from within the chamber of high art, rock 'n' roll musicians were noisily hammering away from the other side. Throughout the 1960s, artists, musicians, writers, and critics who were identified with high culture were eager to assert their approval of rock 'n' roll. No similar enthusiasm about other aspects of popular culture was evident, at least not until the end of the decade. It was rock 'n' roll that spearheaded the successful assault on the ramparts of civilization.

Composers such as Leonard Bernstein and Ned Rorem were especially reverent about the Beatles. Rorem saw the Beatles performing a service similar to that of Pop Art, the popularity of which, at least in part, had been a reaction to the rigorous demands of Abstract Expressionism. The austere complexity of the "serious" composers of the 1950s, such as Elliott Carter, Milton Babbitt, and Arthur Berger, had eclipsed the Art of Song, once well-represented in opera and lieder. If high culture was going to abandon the tradition of musical communication that was Song, argued Rorem, then pop culture would come to the rescue. "The artful tradition of great song has been transferred from elite domains to the Beatles and their offshoots who represent — as any nonspecialized intellectual will tell you — the finest communicable music of our time."[1]

Meanwhile, Susan Sontag, in her now-famous book *Against Interpretation*, was calling for the distinction between high and pop culture to be abandoned. After all, the idea of high culture was so elitist, and these were the egalitarian Sixties. Besides, the feeling prompted by a Robert Rauschenberg painting might be the same as the feeling you get from a song by the Supremes. (Sontag preferred the Supremes to the Beatles; critic Richard Poirier was the most effusive champion of the Fab Four in such environs as the *New York Review of Books*.) Sontag suggested that the purpose of art ought to be the "reorganization of the consciousness," which could more easily be accomplished by rock 'n' roll than by some impenetrable work by Karlheinz Stockhausen. (Parents in the 1960s who complained that the music their kids listened to was just a lot of noise should have been grateful their kids weren't interested in the new classical music.) Sontag was crusading for a turn in the arts to an "anti-cognitive, anti-intellectual" emphasis, and rock fit the needs of the hour.

While Pop Art sprang up in Britain and America in movements independent of one another, rock 'n' roll was a uniquely American invention. But it was very soon given significant new directions from a number of British musicians. The story of the advent of rock cannot be told without Chuck Berry and Elvis Presley, but its subsequent chapters are soon dominated by the influence of the Beatles and the Rolling Stones.

The Pop Art/rock 'n' roll alliance was not just a matter of common cause: it was, for many, a biographical connection. A number of influential British rockers were students in art schools in the 1950s and 1960s, where they were assimilating the new ideas of Pop Art by day and listening to Elvis sing "I'm Left, You're Right, She's Gone" by night. Keith Richards, Pete Townshend, Eric Clapton, Sandy Denny, John Renbourne, and John Lennon were just a few of those students who eventually traded in their air-brushes for microphones or guitars.

Many of these performers, then, had studied Richard Hamilton's 1957 definition of Pop Art (Hamilton would later be asked to design the cover for the Beatles' 1968 "White Album"). Their decision to become rock musicians was thus a very different act than that of Elvis or Little Richard. One doubts that Elvis saw his performances as having some cultural resonance with Claes Oldenburg's oversized cheeseburgers or Andy Warhol's soup cans. But the Beatles, the Rolling Stones, the Who, Cream, and some of the other influential English bands had no little measure of self-consciousness about the cultural moment they were a part of. They were aware (they paid *some* attention to their studies) of the crisis that Pop Art was precipitating in Western culture. They were also very much influenced by the notion of the artist as hero, which had originated in Romanticism and had been propagated by the British art schools. It was this tradition that enabled the seminal English rock musicians to inflect "pop music with bohemian dreams and Romantic fancies and laid out the ideology of 'rock' — on the one hand a new art form, on the other a new community."[2]

Whatever Elvis Presley was, he was *not* a bohemian. A bohemian is someone who enjoys slumming because it involves making a statement about the authenticity of the primitive. Elvis Presley and many of the early rock musicians from the U.S. simply *were* primitive, with no pretensions about statements. They did not have much self-consciousness about establishing a movement. True, Elvis created an unprecedented sensation in American popular culture. But it is doubtful that rock could have had as much of an effect on American society if it had just *been* there, if it had not been accompanied by an argument for its existence that was compelling and timely. The sheer energy of the American originals made rock attractive. The Romantic myth of rock that soon followed made it seem inevitable and unstoppable.

TWIST AND SHOUT

Rock 'n' roll is without question the dominant idiom in modern popular culture. It is not just popular, it is omnipresent. In movie soundtracks, on television commercials, from car radios and boom boxes, at political conventions, in church services, rock is the most common musical form.

Allan Bloom, in *The Closing of the American Mind*, reflected on the overwhelming ubiquity of rock, and the corresponding lack of interest in the music of high culture.

> Classical music is dead among the young. This assertion will, I know, be hotly disputed by many who, unwilling to admit tidal changes, can point to the proliferation on campuses of classes in classical music appreciation and practice, as well as performance groups of all kinds. Their presence is undeniable, but they involve not more than 5 to 10 percent of the students. Classical music is now a special taste, like Greek language or pre-Columbian archeology, not a common culture of reciprocal communication and psychological shorthand. Thirty years ago, most middle-class families made some of the old European music a part of the home, partly because they liked it, partly because they thought it was good for the kids. University students usually had some early emotive association with Beethoven, Chopin and Brahms, which was a permanent part of their their makeup and to which they were likely to respond throughout their lives. This was probably the only regularly recognizable class distinction between educated and uneducated in America. Many, or even most, of the young people of that generation also swung with Benny Goodman, but with an element of self-consciousness — to be hip, to prove they weren't snobs, to show solidarity with the democratic ideal of a pop culture out of which would grow a new high culture. So there remained a class distinction between high and low, although private taste was beginning to create doubts about whether one really liked the high very much. But all that has changed. Rock music is as unquestioned and unproblematic as the air the students breathe, and very few have any acquaintance at all with classical music.[3]

Bloom's observation that rock is "unquestioned and unproblematic" is most interesting. The legitimacy or propriety of many other cultural activities are readily questioned (or at least questionable) by students. Smoking, drinking, cheating, fornicating, marrying, watching television, reading pornography, eating certain foods, playing video games, believing in God: one could probably find a number of students who would be willing to discuss the merits and demerits of any of these choices, who could sense how choosing to do any one of these things was a serious matter. One could also easily establish a discussion about choosing to attend the opera or ballet, to read Greek tragedies, or to listen to medieval music. Of course, such endeavors "aren't for everyone," they are a matter of "taste," but a case could be made that such activities are worthy.

But rock is apparently not something modern students have a taste for, except in the sense that they have a taste for air. Consider the following:

> In 1976, two social scientists at Temple University wanted to investigate students' physical and emotional reactions to rock. They had no difficulty locating an experimental group of fifty-six rock enthusiasts for their study, but when they tried to form a control group, "a significant sample could not be found who disliked hard rock music."[4]

Saying that rock music is the dominant idiom of popular culture may seem a bit simplistic. After all, what kind of rock do I have in mind? There *are* dozens of varieties of rock music, but, as Billy Joel might say, "It's still rock 'n' roll to me." All of those styles are still somehow rock. If there are many rooms in the house of rock, there is a single rock *myth*, and the dominance of rock in popular culture is due to the dominance of the rock myth, not of a particular sound.

The essence of that myth was that rock would offer a form of spiritual deliverance by providing a superior *form of knowledge*, a form that was immediate rather than reflective, physical rather than mental, and emotional rather than volitional.

SOUL MAN

In 1971, *Rolling Stone* editor Jann Wenner offered this analysis of the editorial philosophy of his magazine.

Rolling Stone was founded and continues to operate in the belief that rock 'n' roll music is the energy center for all sorts of changes revolving rapidly around us: social, political, cultural, however you want to describe them. The fact is for many of us who've grown up since World War II, rock 'n' roll provided the first revolutionary insight into who we are and where we are at in this country: our first discovery that behind the plasticized myth of what we had been told was the United States, behind that Eisenhower-Walt Disney-Doris Day facade was a real America: funky, violent, deeply divided, despairing, exultant, rooted in rich historical tradition and ethnic variety.[5]

Several things are notable about Wenner's remarks. First, he characterizes rock as a means of insight about America. He must mean that the sensibility of rock communicated something about the society. But did it simply communicate something about those who listened to it? Did they feel funky, violent, etc., resonate with the music, and project that feeling out beyond themselves?

Second, in what sense could one say that those things represented by Eisenhower, Walt Disney, and Doris Day are not "real"? Perhaps they were not real because they were not "revolutionary." Or perhaps they were not real because they weren't funky, violent, etc.

Finally, concerning the "rich historical tradition and ethnic variety" communicated by rock, this man is certainly not talking about discovering in rock something about the heritage of Irish, Polish, Italian, or Norwegian Americans. He is talking about black Americans. There is a slightly racist assumption here that black America was more real than white America. But as we shall see, in that assumption is the key to the myth of rock 'n' roll.

In his 1970 manifesto for the New Age, *The Greening of America*, Charles A. Reich wrote about the dawning of a new consciousness in American culture (in Reich's scenario it was called Consciousness III).

Consciousness III starts with self. In contrast to Consciousness II, which accepts society, the public interest, and institutions as the primary reality, III declares that the individual self is the only true reality. Thus it returns to the earlier America: "Myself I sing." The first commandment is: thou shalt not do violence to thyself.[6]

Note the self-centeredness and the pantheism involved in this "higher" consciousness. Reich was also relativistic: his second commandment is "No one judges anyone else."[7] In addition, Reich's new consciousness was profoundly irrational, and was to be mediated by rock, which had injected a pulsing new energy into the culture.

Not even the turbulent fury of Beethoven's Ninth Symphony can compete for sheer energy with the Rolling Stones. Compared to the new music, earlier popular songs seem escapist and soft, jazz seems cerebral, classical music seems dainty or mushy; these epithets are surely undeserved, but the driving, screaming, crying, bitter-happy-sad heights and depths and motion of the new music adds a dimension unknown in any earlier western music. The older music was essentially intellectual; it was located in the mind and in the feelings known to the mind; the new music rocks the whole body, and penetrates the soul.[8]

The nature of rock's new form of knowledge was sensational rather than rational. Reich's celebration of experience in this way is reminiscent of Lord Byron, the model Romantic, who once wrote: "The great object of life is Sensation — to feel that we exist — even though in pain — it is this 'craving void' which drives us to Gaming — to Battle — to Travel — to intemperate but keenly felt pursuits of every description."[9]

If it seems a long way from Lord Byron to David Byrne, let's consider how rock and Romanticism might fit in a family tree. Starting back a few generations, the Enlightenment begat two warring siblings: the boisterous boy Industrialism and his melancholy half-sister Romanticism. Their incestuous, unhappy union brought forth early Modernism, and while still young, Modernism begat twin brothers: the contemplative, smooth man of the tradition-haunted avant-garde (Eliot, Stravinsky, Abstract Expressionism), and the frenetic, hairy man of the radical avant-garde (Dada, Dali, Pop Art). There is a good case to be made that the radical avant-garde had the more legitimate claim to the family name. Its temperament fulfilled the experimental, primitivist longings of Modernism, it was irrational like Romanticism, and it had the industrialist's love of machines.

Rock 'n' roll comes from the same family tree. It is a creation of popular culture, and so has ancestral roots in the Industrial Revolution which made mass culture possible and which precipitated the response of Modernism. But rock, as we shall see, also has the thick, hot blood of Romanticism in its veins. It is therefore genetically close to the radical avant-garde. As we saw in the last chapter, the aesthetic of Pop Art and that of popular culture were virtually identical. They are, after all, kissin' kin. No wonder they were able to team up so effectively in the 1960s.

MAGICAL MYSTERY TOUR

Romanticism was a reaction to the rationalism of the Enlightenment. Remember Jacques Barzun's analysis: "When life has been stripped and sanitized by reason — or at least by discourse that sounds like reason — the unsatisfied desires that are left over must find some outlet."[10] The Romantics rebelled against the effort "to subject all of life to reason, and thus to mechanize and demean it."[11] Isaac Newton became a symbol of such rationalistic narrowness. William Blake's *Newton* depicts the scientist "trying to fathom the world by means of a pair of compasses, that is, by measurement and 'reason' alone."[12]

The Romantics were right to object to Rationalism. Certainly all of creation cannot be comprehended (in the sense of contained as well as understood) by reason. There are mysteries about the creation and about the Creator that surpass reason's limits. But the Romantic solution to the limitations of

Rationalism was just as inadequate. While it properly insisted on a realm of transcendence beyond the material world (usually expressed in terms of a pursuit of the Infinite), Romanticism usually did not think of the transcendent in terms of an infinite and personal God. It also erred in exhibiting a strong sense of the *primacy of the irrational* in human life. To say that creation cannot be fully comprehended by reason is *not* to say that it is irrational.

Another attribute of Romanticism was its stressing of the individual and the particular as opposed to the general, which in turn led to its tendency toward pantheism, of seeing every individual as a mere particularization of "a greater Whole, Spirit, or Universe."[13] This pantheism was evident in the nature mysticism of many Romantics. It also affected Protestant theology. Friedrich Schleiermacher, the earliest significant proponent of what became known as theological Liberalism, was strongly influenced by Romanticism. Schleiermacher defined true religion as a "sense and taste for the Infinite," which was to be found in man's inmost soul, in "feeling." According to Schleiermacher, "Each individual was a unique embodiment of the All, and experienced the All in his own unique way."[14]

Romanticism, then, fostered an emphasis on instinct, a tendency toward irrationality, and a sympathy with pantheism. Out of these attributes, it is not surprising to discover two other characteristics of Romanticism: its *celebration of youth* and its belief that a *return to the primitive* was a means of recovering human integrity. Both children and primitive cultures are instinctual rather than reflective. They are not troubled by irrational superstitions. Children tend to be self-centered, while primitive peoples are often pantheistic; both of these options are ways of positing that the self is the center of the Universe, that it has deep inner resources that hold the key to the meaning of existence.

Romanticism passed each of these attributes on to the radical avant-garde of Modernism. And each of them also is very prominent in the heart of rock 'n' roll.

In his book *The Triumph of Vulgarity: Rock Music in the Mirror of Romanticism*,[15] Robert Pattison argues quite persuasively that "nineteenth-century Romanticism lives on in the mass culture of the twentieth century,"[16] especially in rock 'n' roll. If rock is the dominant idiom of popular culture, it is worth taking some time to consider some of the details of Pattison's argument to see how the worldview of Romanticism has resurfaced in a surprising form.

One of the ideas that orders Pattison's argument is that of vulgarity. To be vulgar is to to be crude and noisy, to lack reason, contemplation, and any sense of the transcendent. "In its pure form," argues Pattison, "Romantic pantheism encourages vulgarity."[17] It does so because it despises the mechanisms of cultivation. The Romantics believed that man is born innocent and becomes corrupted through exposure to culture. The "God" in man becomes obscured by the accretions of "civilized" culture. Hence, Romantic pantheism tends to encourage the idea that the most primitive forms of human culture are superior forms. A commitment to primitivism determines a number of other preferences: "authenticity over artifice, expression over classical restraint, invention over imitation, the natural over the civilized, the intuitive over the rational, the raw over the refined."[18] It is easy to see how celebrating the primitive would encourage a toleration of vulgarity. If the Noble Savage is the highest form of man, you can hardly protest if his table manners are deplorable.

The high-culture version of Romanticism could never bring itself to acknowledge "the vulgarity inherent in its own premises." For over a century, it lived in tension with its premises, although the bohemianism of some Romantics and many Modernists was an early, if tentative, endorsement of vulgarity. But as we have seen, with the wall between popular culture and high culture having been eliminated, *everyone* can be vulgar.

LET'S GET PRIMITIVE

Vulgarity is a *product* of primitivism, not a synonym. There are other ways in which rock is expressive of the Romantic myth of the primitive. Pattison explains that this myth was one of the reactions to life in industrialized society. The story of Tarzan is one setting of that myth, the man raised by apes, swinging happily through the trees, more in tune with nature than St. Francis, talking to elephants and tigers, and finally offering his companion Jane more happiness than she could ever know in her stuffy, "civilized" world.

A more sophisticated and theoretical development of the primitivist ideology was stated by Jean-Jacques Rousseau, as early as 1762, in his *Social Contract*. Rousseau's philosophy held that

> a man is free when he develops according to the dictates of nature. If he can avoid polluting contacts with civilization, he will grow up with his authenticity intact. Civilization is corrupt because it takes natural men who are at one with nature and makes them smaller, turning citizens of the universe into mere Frenchmen, for instance, or reducing cosmic wisdom to the cliches of party platforms. All social associations are bad because they diminish the human wholeness of their members. In a perfect society, says Rousseau, men will avoid all associations and retain their primitive virtue.[19]

The Tahitians in Paul Gauguin's painting are another expression of the primitivist myth. Gauguin was a true believer in the nineteenth-century myth of the Noble Savage, "living in blissful innocence in the fruitful bosom of nature."[20] Throughout the 1880s, Gauguin, a young banker who moved in a literary and artistic set, developed a passionate hatred of bourgeois existence. In 1891 he finally set sail for Tahiti, taking along brushes, canvas, and paint, as well as two mandolins and a guitar for Romantic evenings. "These nymphs," he wrote back to friends in France, "I want to perpetuate them, with their golden skins, their searching animal odour, their tropical savours."[21]

There are also Noble Savages outside of art. Much of the reverence accorded Native Americans in the past two decades is certainly the result from a late-1960s brand of primitivism, the same brand that endorsed organic gardening and natural materials in clothing.

The myth of rock, argues Robert Pattison, involves the assumption that music influenced by *blacks* is necessarily more natural, more organic, because blacks are more primitive. "Blacks become the great primal source of all goodness. . . . The black man is thought to have 'natural rhythm' generated by the world's primal energy, and white, middle-class rock wants it. Rock has room for other ideals of the primitive, but none of these is dogmatically necessary for the music. The black primitive is."[22]

GIVE THE DRUMMER SOME

Pattison notes that the tradition of white people using blacks' experience "as a canvas on which to paint their Romantic portraits of life in a state of nature" is centuries old. What the rock myth added was the belief that rhythm, especially in dance, was the essence of black life. Remember Charles Reich's claim that "the new music rocks the whole body, and penetrates the soul." The myth of rock begins in the primitivist/pantheist assertion that African-Americans are closer to the center of things, and that their organic spirituality is tied to the rhythms that shaped rock 'n' roll. This myth is nowhere more fully stated than in two articles by Michael Ventura, originally published in the progressive *L.A. Weekly*.[23]

Ventura begins by asserting that the African religions out of which rock evolved held "the conviction that religious worship is a *bodily* celebration, a dance of the entire community."[24] This is very important to Ventura because he is convinced that what is ailing Western civilization is the "mind-body split" which was "codified by Christianism." (Ventura's hatred of Christianity is evident in the fact that he constantly uses the demeaning term "Christianism.") In the "Christianist" West, people were taught that one should *reasonably* control one's bodily impulses, that one should order one's life by the reflection of the mind, not by the instincts of the body. One of the reasons this is so bad, in Ventura's view, is that such rationalism not only inhibits spontaneity, it prevents the spirit world from taking possession of one's body and soul. That is a great loss for Western man.

But the primitive African was spared this horrible handicap:

The mind-body split that governs European thought seems never to have entered African religion, African consciousness

— at least not until imported there by missionaries. To meditate was to dance. Hence in this culture the drum is so sacred an instrument that some are built only for display. They are too holy to touch.[25]

The African "metaphysic" was actually communicated through music, claims Ventura, most powerfully through the music associated with Voodoo in Haiti and, eventually, New Orleans.

Jazz and rock 'n' roll would evolve from Voodoo, carrying within them the metaphysical antidote that would aid many a twentieth-century Westerner from both the ravages of the mind-body split codified by Christianism, and the onslaught of technology. The twentieth century would dance as no other had, and, through that dance, secrets would be passed.[26]

Ironically, the prophet of those hidden mysteries was a *white* boy named Elvis, "a gash in the Western nature of things."[27] Ventura says that Presley's arrival in the culture was an advent in the fullness of time; he brought with him an ancient way of knowledge that created all of the movements of the 1960s, because it established a sense of spiritual community among people who were caught up in the music, a community that agreed with the African metaphysic against the Western one.

Ventura's claims are about half right. Yes, rock created a sense of spiritual community that fostered a number of cultural, social, and political movements. But did its ability to do that reside in its communication of secrets from the dark but enlightened continent to white, middle-class youth?

Ventura seems to be guilty of projecting his notions of primitivism and pantheism on the screen of black experience. John Miller Chernoff, an American sociologist who spent two years in Africa learning to play a drum, argues that while music plays a part in some of the cultic rituals of certain African religions, in general the social role of music in African life does not at all resemble a non-stop "Soul Train."

Our word "ecstatic," which some people like to apply to African music, means literally from its Greek origins, "extended out of the state one was in," and the word could not be more inappropriate to describe African music in general. The feelings the music brings may be exhilarating but not overpowering, intense but not frenzied. Ecstasy as we see it would imply for most Africans a separation from all that is good and beautiful, and generally, in fact, any such loss of control is viewed by them as tasteless, ridiculous, or even sinful.[28]

So even if there is something to Ventura's idea about the power of rock 'n' roll to create a new sensibility (an idea which he shares with countless commentators on rock and on the cultural history of the 1960s), that power may really have nothing to do with Africa. It is not localized or tied to a particular race. Rather, it is tied to the interplay between the body and the imagination. The music may well have some intrinsic qualities that have a hedonistic appeal. But what the rock myth needs is the moral argument that the impulses prompted by the music were pure and noble because they were the product of some more enlightened culture.

Robert Pattison offers some perspective on this:

Black music has supplied the raw material for rock, but there is no reason to suppose that blacks share the same Romantic preoccupations necessary for rock, and some reason to suppose that they do not. When whites respond to black music, they move to the jungle rhythms of their Romantic imagination, not to any objective force. In South Africa, a black group called Amampondo has tried to preserve the tribal music of the continent. The *New York Times* reports that their leader, Dizu Plaatjies, the son of a witchdoctor, was puzzled by the different responses of whites and blacks to the group's music. "Black people, Mr. Plaatjies said, are the most difficult to please or to get to participate. Whites, however, frequently leap into the aisles to dance in a manner they perhaps consider African." There is nothing in the modern world more primitive than a white man in the grip of his own Romantic sensibilities.[29]

There were some powerful historical and political forces at work as the rock era dawned, forces which enhanced the appeal of primitivism, and hence of the myth of rock. The civil rights movement created a new sympathy on the part of many white Americans for the plight of blacks, and a new sense of guilt for somehow having been responsible for the horrors of slavery and its aftermath. As society began to move to make restitution through civil rights laws, so many whites felt moved to make personal atonement, in some cases by condemning Western culture and praising non-Western values. To counterbalance the racism of America, many whites became racists toward their own race. Black *was* beautiful, and the white race was a sickness unto death.

A similar dynamic was operating on an international scale, with many Westerners practicing a new "religion of compassionate sympathy"[30] for all suffering people everywhere. Often these people came from more primitive societies, and celebration of their moral superiority because they were primitive only enhanced their status as victims. Such expressions of "Third-Worldism" had a religious component as well. As artist Ted Prescott has written, many Westerners suffer

a feeling of guilt for the past destruction of primitive cultures by colonial powers, and the continuing disappearance of the primitive as it is absorbed into the industrial world. Having rejected Christian teaching about the transcendence of God, secularized society still longs for some shred of mystery and magic. Having denied the truth of Genesis as an explanation of man's origin, modern thinkers have a great need to preserve the primitive as a link to some original meaning in human experience.[31]

DON'T KNOW MUCH ABOUT HISTORY

The influential English rock musicians were also influenced by Eastern pantheism. The Beatles were, for a short but much celebrated period, disciples of the Maharishi Mahesh Yogi, and ended up playing with sitars and using Indian musical forms on a few albums. Meanwhile, guitarist John McLaughlin formed the Mahavishnu Orchestra and produced such albums as *Visions of the Emerald Beyond* and *Between Nothingness and Eternity*. Given the significant Indian population in Britain, "Indians are for Brits an available form of primitivism,"[32] argues Pattison, and since the English can feel just as guilty about the way their race has treated the Indians as white Americans can about the way blacks have been treated here, another emotional component is added to the primitivism.

But the most powerful explanation for rock's attraction to India is the long-standing place that India has had in the Romantic imagination. Walt Whitman, Ralph Waldo Emerson, Alfred Lord, Tennyson, and E. M. Forster "are only the best-known names associated with a Romantic adulation of Eastern wisdom," reports Pattison.[33] India was the source of pantheistic enlightenment. Simply by listening to Ravi Shankar one could participate in the music of the spheres. (Image what energy could have been unleashed in the cosmos if Ravi Shankar could have made an album with Bo Diddley! Awesome!)

The India of Romantic myth has as much to do with the real place as the Africa of the rock myth does. But the Romantic myth of rock is not interested in real places or real times, for this myth is finally pantheistic. Who needs reality in space and time when you have the whole world in your heart? Pattison points out that

> Emerson announced the pantheist program when he said, "There is properly no history, only biography." Where the self is all in all, the disparate parts of time contained in history books are mere appearance. Biography, the study of the self, is the reality of the universe, which is only the endless variation of self in its infinite incarnations.[34]

Or, as the Ramones put it:

I don't care about history,
That's not where I want to be —
I just wanna have some kicks.[35]

And finally, from Chuck Berry:

Hail, hail, rock 'n' roll,
   Deliver me from days of old,
Long live rock 'n' roll
   The beat of the drums loud and bold.[36]

I SECOND THAT EMOTION

So far we have said little about two other attributes that rock has in common with Romanticism: its appeal to instinct and irrationality, and its celebration of youth. As Pattison notes: "Rock lyrics are suffused with the language of emotion: *need, want,* and *feel* are the building blocks of its abstract vocabulary. Logic and reason are everywhere associated with the loss of youth and the death of vitality."[37] He cites as an example Supertramp's "The Logical Song":

When I was young, it seemed that life was so wonderful,
A miracle, oh it was beautiful, magical. . . .
But then they sent me away to teach me how to be
   sensible,
Logical, responsible, practical,
And they showed me a world where I could be so
   dependable,
Clinical, intellectual, cynical.[38]

Not only do rock lyrics denigrate reason, but the way rock is usually experienced discourages any kind of careful reflection. Much of the time, rock (like most popular music) is used to cover over silence. Whether in a car, on a bus, or when walking, rock music serves for its listeners as a kind of personal sound track, enlivening tedious activities with excitement, much the same way that film and television scores enliven boring passages with exciting music. Time that could be spent thinking is thus spent listening and daydreaming.

Of course, any kind of music can be used this way. But most rock is produced to be used *only* this way. It is generally intended to be *used*, not *received*. Jazz, on the other hand, is more complex, sometimes so complex that it actually *discourages* casual listening.

Another factor in rock's discouragement of thoughtfulness is the social pressure, especially on young listeners, to be up on all the latest tunes, as well as on all the latest rock gossip, the sort of stuff MTV VJs specialize in. I can remember listening to the radio many evenings (while allegedly doing my homework) so I could be conversant about what was the most important shared experience among my peers.

The denigration of reason and the elevation of instinct is characteristic of rock's pantheistic character. "When the pantheist equates self and God," observes Pattison, "he demotes thought to a secondary role in the universe and elevates feeling as the fundamental way of knowing."[39] Remember that Susan Sontag talked about rock involving a "reorganization of the consciousness," that *Rolling Stone's* Jann Wenner talked about its "revolutionary insights," and that Charles Reich spoke of its capability to "rock the whole body and penetrate the soul." As Daniel Bell noted, the 1960s were filled with calls to surrender to "one form or another of pre-rational spontaneity." Similar to Reich's Consciousness III was Theodore Roszak's "shamanistic vision."

> Nothing less is required than the subversion of the scientific world view with its entrenched commitment to an egocentric and cerebral mode of consciousness. In its place, there must be a new culture in which the non-intellective capacities of personality — those capacities that take fire from visionary splendor and the experience of human communion — become the arbiters of the true, the good, and the beautiful.[40]

Rock was a music made to order for this new cultural vision. Bursting onto the scene when it did, it thus had a remarkably wide appeal: it had a natural appeal to youth, who enjoy noisy, emotional, and sensual displays. But it also fulfilled the prescription of many sophisticated Western adults, for whom the tradition of high culture had become exhausted, and who were looking for liberation in experience.

The fact that rock appealed to youth contributed to its myth. The narcissistic hero of nineteenth-century Romanticism was also ever young and ever new. Dick Clark's longevity as the premier impresario of rock is a symbol of rock's Peter Pan myth of eternal youth. The sight and sound of the Beach Boys ("Boys?" These guys are almost ready for Social Security) pretending they still belong on the beach impressing the young bimbos is an embodiment of the Romantic myth of youth.

YOU BELONG TO THE CITY

Not so long ago, within Christian circles rock was regarded as a much more dubious cultural activity than it is today. The usual line offered in defense of rock 'n' roll was, "But it has so much energy." What was rarely asked in response was why the experience of energy was intrinsically a good thing.

Mere energy, undirected and purposeless, is generally regarded as a nuisance. Mere energy is the stuff of insomnia, not creativity. It is what parents and teachers lament in hyperactive children. Energy is only an asset when it can be directed toward a task.

Toward what sort of task does the energy of rock apply itself? One of the more obvious outlets for rock's energy is sex. This theme is a very familiar one, and is the staple of Christian criticism of rock. But it is usually an argument advanced only in the interests of preserving chastity. Rock's excessive sexual preoccupations pose a much more fundamental question: Is rock's eroticism (especially in its most excessive forms) not only immoral but idolatrous? Is sexual pleasure made into a false god?

Robert Pattison suggests that a pantheistic theme is evident here as well, using language that makes one wonder if he's been reading Bill Bright in between listening to AC/DC and the Ramones:

> The pantheist's desire to usurp God's throne and substitute self in His place is naturally erotic. The sex drive is the most obvious case of the self expanding its boundaries in what

Blake calls "continual gyrations" to include more territory, and the widening circle of inclusion that begins with sex ends with God obliterated. . . . Rock belongs in the Romantic tradition that rejoices in the sex drive as a leading ingredient in the energy that casts off self-limitation in its quest for the infinite. This energy may be revolutionary or perverse. John Lennon writes, "Why don't we do it in the road," John Cougar embroiders the tradition of de Sade and Swinburne when he sings that love "hurts so good."[41]

Clearly this is not the energy the Christian defenders of rock have in mind.

I believe what they do have in mind is something more like the energy stimulated by athletic activity. But there, too, we have a problem. For the rush of adrenaline and the soaring of pulse rate for a fullback heading for a goal line or a basketball forward in a fast break has a *goal*, and the means and the style for discharging that energy are determined by the end in view. The energy stimulated by rock certainly has an end for the players: it's hard work playing in the E Street Band every night. (George Will once remarked that backstage at a Springsteen concert, one was more likely to catch the odor of Ben-Gay than pot.)

If you're not actually in the band, you can pretend you are. One of the reasons many rock fans privately simulate the frenzied playing of a guitarist or the rapid-fire hammering of a drummer is that if you're not dancing, you have to do *something*. Mimicking the motions of the players serves to use some of that energy, as well as serving the fantasy of being one of the band members. Singing also works, especially if you pretend you're holding a microphone.

This activity is not entirely unlike that of a classical music fan who conducts the choral movement in Beethoven's "Ninth," or who cues the cannon in the "1812 Overture." But some differences are suggested by the fantasy microphone. The person conducting the chorus rarely if ever thinks of himself as pretending to be Maestro Herbert von Karajan or Leonard Bernstein. In those moments of energetic exuberance, it is the *music* that is being entered into, not the *performance*. But the rock fan seems to be more interested in entering the performance, in pretending to be the guitarist or drummer or singer. Facial movements, gestures, even acknowledgment of an imaginary audience are often a part of this pantomime.

If this analysis is right (and I may be stretching a wee bit, but not too much), it would seem to suggest that the energy of rock is (in Pattison's phrase) "the energy that drives the self." It is not, like the energy of the athlete, an energy that is consumed in the pursuit of a task, but rather energy that stokes the pursuit of the self.

Pattison says that according to the pantheistic vision of rock, "Cars, parties, and cities are all expressions of that fundamental energy by which the self creates the universe." Cars, parties, and cities are all common in the scenarios of rock lyrics. One doesn't hear many rock songs about walking in the country, but there are a lot about T-birds, wild parties, and urban nights. Cars, parties, and cities are also places where the performance of rock seems naturally situated.

The car is one of the great instruments of self-definition in America, perhaps the greatest. And no one using a car to assert something about self-identity drives a slow car. Parties are a context for playing a role, for letting down your hair and being who you can't quite be day in and day out, for casual and experimental liaisons. Cities are the locale where the malleability of the self can be realized. Cities are where people from the country and the suburbs go to "find themselves."

The energy of rock, tied to cars, parties, and cities, is thereby tied to a context in which people try to remake themselves by their own standards. The self *is* the center of the universe in a fast car. Everything *does* revolve around you at a great party. The city's possibilities are there for you to exploit, no questions asked.

GOD: NUMBER ONE WITH A BULLET

Much of what has been said in this chapter is open to question. After all, as someone once said, we're not talking about batting averages. If I could prove all of the assertions made here *scien-*

tifically, I might be tempted to get a job in marketing. But I hope that I have at least succeeded in suggesting that rock is *problematic*, in demonstrating that serious questions can be raised about rock's unquestioned dominance of our culture and, for some of us, of our lives.

Asserting that the myth of rock is pantheistic in no way means that people who play or listen to rock are all pantheists. But since we are *all* tempted to some form of idolatry, it is helpful to know where we need to erect some defenses. If the rock myth *does* involve the tacit endorsement of pantheistic, primitivistic celebration of the self and the senses, there must be something in the music that somehow corresponds to the myth. It is not likely that rock will make *professing* pantheists out of many people, but its place in our society does pose some other challenges. Robert Pattison suggests that rock's threat to religion is that it forces "churches to compete [with rock-dominated culture] on the basis of their ability to titillate the instincts of their worshippers," thereby making religious leaders

> entrepreneurs of emotional stimulation. Once God becomes a commodity for self-gratification, his fortunes depend on the vagaries of the emotional marketplace, and his claim to command allegiance on the basis of omnipotence or omniscience vanishes in a blaze of solipsism as his priests and shamans pander to the feeling, not the faith, of their customers.[42]

How much of the liturgical and educational life of our churches has been influenced by this need for emotional stimulation, whether or not the music we sing sounds at all like rock? How many sermons are shaped by the necessity of communicating to a culture dominated by this new sensibility?

Such questions are especially relevant when we consider a troubling historical fact. At the time rock was asserting the new dominance of an instinct-driven popular culture in American society, conservative Protestants were trying to assess two phenomena within their ranks: the Jesus People and the charismatic movement. The Jesus People were essentially Christian hippies, an unorganized assortment of relatively new believers who were adamant in their eagerness to construct their fellowship and wor-ship according to the sensibility of the counterculture. They were "contextualizing" the gospel in the setting of Consciousness III.

Today the charismatic movement is almost "unproblemat-ic" in evangelical circles, but it was a hotly debated issue during the late 1960s and into the 1970s. It is at least a curious thing that this was exactly the time that Charles A. Reich was calling for Consciousness III and Theodore Roszak was extolling "the non-intellective capacities of personality — those capacities that take fire from visionary splendor and the experience of human communion" as "the arbiters of the true, the good, and the beau-tiful."

The charismatic claim was that non-intellective bodily and emotional forms of communication from God were a central aspect of true piety. One must ask to what extent the controversy over this claim was settled by the power of exegetical proof from the Scriptures, and to what extent the controversy simply died down because the new cultural sensibility of instinctiveness made it difficult to sustain *any* argument, especially an argument con-cerning ecstatic utterance.

One must also ask to what extent the *popularity* of the charismatic claim is due to the work of the *Heiliger Geist* (Holy Spirit) and how much was simply the effect of the *Zeitgeist*. A personal anecdote is in order. I remember a young woman exclaiming to me in the early 1970s how wonderful it was that she had been filled by the Holy Spirit, because she didn't have to *think* about her faith any more. That probably was not orthodox even by the standards of the charismatic church she attended, but she didn't seem to mind. And why did she *assume* that it was wonderful not to have to think about her faith? Was it because she had come of age in the 1960s and was influenced by the fash-ionable preference for pre-rational spontaneity?

The evangelical churches in America by and large consented to the legitimacy of the charismatic claim at about the same time they stopped fussing about rock 'n' roll. To be sure, there are still many Christians uncomfortable with both, but they are generally relegated to the fringes. They are simply uptight; and since the advent of Consciousness III, uptight is *not* where you want to be.

POPULAR CULTURE'S MEDIUM: THE ENTERTAINMENT APPLIANCE

TELEVISION WON

The *New York Times* for Tuesday, March 7, 1989 brought us one of those moments in journalism where the real story is a matter of collage rather than reportage. In the fourth and fifth columns of page 8 there was a story on what was at the time a familiar controversy. The headline read: "News Shows with Ads Are Tested in 6 Schools."

The story was about the first broadcast of a pilot for a short daily television news show designed to be used in junior and senior high school classrooms. The pilot was produced by a company called Whittle Communications in Knoxville, Tennessee, and distributed by satellite to six schools. The company hoped to have the show, called "Channel One," placed in eight thousand schools within eighteen months. While there is nothing new about classroom use of TV, the hook here is that this show has commercials, and that makes a lot of people upset. "In return for thousands of dollars of free equipment, including the 25-inch color television sets, videocassette recorders and satellite dishes," the *Times* reported, "the schools agree to make the 12-minute program required viewing for all students."

It was the prospect of students being coerced to watch the commercials (for Levis, Snickers, and other teen-consumables) that had many critics, including "a number of leading educators," up in arms, announcing press conferences and calling reporters. Less than a week earlier, Chris Whittle, who will no doubt make a lot of money if this project works, defended "Channel One" in a piece published on the Op-Ed page of the *Times*, essentially saying that if government funds couldn't meet the requirements of schools who want to provide information about current events for classroom use, then the private sector would help.

Directly underneath this story was a shorter, happier report accompanied by a photo of smiling Barbara Bush, a young black girl and a young white girl on her lap. This headline announced: "Barbara Bush Announces Formation of Literacy Foundation." It seems that twenty-three million adult Americans are functionally illiterate, "lacking basic skills beyond a fourth-grade level, experts in the field estimate. Another 35 million are semi-literate, lacking skills beyond the eighth-grade level." That's fifty-eight million adults, incapable of grasping, for example, the meaning and consequences of most of the prose on the Op-Ed page of the *Times*. The Barbara Bush Foundation for Family Literacy will "stress 'intergenerational activities,' and target the family as the key to establishing literacy as 'a universal value in the nation,' Mrs. Bush said." Hence the kids on her lap.

The story between the stories here is that while the First Lady is raising funds to teach almost sixty million adults how to read, the people who should have taught them to read in the first place have wholeheartedly accepted the dominance of television in education, an instrument that encourages illiteracy. *None* of the "leading educators" cited in this story (or in any other story I could find) raised any questions about the suitability of relying on television as the primary means of providing information in a classroom. What bothered them was the commercials.

What struck me as especially ironic about the juxtaposition of these two stories was the memory of my own high school experience with "current events." During my senior year, we were given the option (but strongly encouraged by our social studies teacher) of subscribing to the *New York Times* (delivered at school at special student rates). The administrators and faculty felt that the best way to help us stay informed was to get us to *read*. There were ads in the editions of the *Times* we received, but as I recall, no one objected to our being pressured (if not coerced) to read it every day.

Today television has become the assumed medium for just about everything. Like rock 'n' roll, it is no longer problematic. Critic Mark Crispin Miller suggests that one of the most important facts about television is that no one complains about it any more. There had been protests about television almost since its invention, and jeremiads about radio, mass journalism, and advertising before that. "By the late Seventies, however, there were virtually no more public outcries from a critical intelligentsia, but only TV's triumphal flow."[1] Miller suggests that the critics had been silenced because television "was no longer a mere stain or imposition on some preexisting cultural environment, but had become the environment."[2]

Of course, one could argue that Miller's own book disproves his thesis, as does Jerry Mander's 1977 *Four Arguments for the Elimination of Television*, Neil Postman's 1985 *Amusing Ourselves to Death*, Marie Winn's revised edition of *The Plug-In Drug*, also published in 1985, and several other titles. But these are voices crying in the flickering shadows of a vast wasteland. None of the "leading educators" seem willing to endorse arguments such as Neil Postman's or Marie Winn's, and neither do many political or religious figures. The educators are trying to teach children raised on "Sesame Street," a program which teaches more about being entertained than about the alphabet. The politicians cannot get elected without television's assistance, and the religious leaders are as interested in ratings as anyone else.

Perhaps this is too cynical. Perhaps they are motivated more by a sense of the common good, and they all realize that television is the only thing holding our culture together. It *is* our culture. Miller reflects on how ignoring television is the modern equivalent of monasticism:

Certainly you could choose not to own a television set, but such refusal would condemn you to a life of touristic ignorance, for TV had now become the native language. While variously emulating TV's look and tempo, the other media — films, books, magazines, newspapers — were also referring endlessly to TV's ephemeral content: the only referent of our "public discourse" in the Eighties, when TV finally became the one subject of stand-up comedy, the context of rock music, a frequent news item, a common talk show topic, the scene and arbiter of politics and the major source of political rhetoric ("Where's the beef?" "How do you spell relief?" "We make money the old-fashioned way," etc.).[3]

Television is thus not simply the dominant medium of *popular* culture, it is the single most significant shared reality in our entire society. Christendom was defined as a region dominated by Christianity. Not all citizens of Christendom were Christians, but all understood it, all were influenced by its teaching, all institutions had to contend with it. Christianity was the one great assumption of Christendom. I can think of no entity today capable of such a culturally unifying role except television. In television, we live and move and have our being.

IDOL TIME

Media guru Tony Schwartz describes the electronic media as "the second god."[4] Of course, we should recognize that Schwartz has a vested interest in hawking such a metaphor. After all, if radio and television are a god, then Tony Schwartz is the second Moses. But there is something sound about the analogy. If not omnipresent, the electronic media are anywhere we want them to be. If not omnipotent, they have substantial social and political power. If not omniscient, they are nonetheless the source of all sorts of knowledge for many people. If not eternal, they do (thanks to oldies stations and reruns on cable) have a certain timelessness.

But more consequential than these superficial analogies is the fact that the media, especially television, serve in our culture a role once reserved for God: the role of defining reality. According to Biblical Christianity, it is God's will and God's word that establishes the meaning and significance of all things. In Christendom, God was publicly recognized as the ultimate arbiter and judge of all things.

Television as a cultural force has no "will," and says only what programmers want it to (or so they think). But the *form* of television, the *way* it communicates, predetermines what is and (more significantly) what is not communicated. Schubert's "Trout" Quintet played by a kazoo band is not really the same piece of music Schubert composed. If you lived in a place where the only musical ensemble that was allowed to play in public was a kazoo band, the reality of Schubert's music, and of most music, would be redefined. It would not be perceived as it ought to be. Its nature would be obscured by the medium. In a somewhat analogous way, television limits the publicly available definitions of reality.

Because of the way television works, if the content of every television program was consistent with a Christian worldview, but television was still as pervasive as it is today, I believe it would still pose serious problems for Christians.

The dominant form of communication in our culture is visual rather than verbal. The Image rather than the Word is the basic unit of communication. More people rely more often on images for knowledge about the world than ever before, thanks in large measure, but not exclusively, to television. This fact may seem innocuous, but it has profound consequences.

Consider the history of magazines, for example. Jacques Ellul notes that sometime in the 1950s a dramatic shift began to take place.

> Previously images were mere illustrations of a dominant text. Language was by far the most important element, and in addition there were images to make the text's content more explicit and hold the reader's attention. This was their sole purpose. Now the situation is reversed: the image contains everything. And as we turn the pages we follow a sequence of images, making use of a completely different mental operation.[5]

Billboards, packaging design, industrial design, films, newspapers, photographs: all of the modern objects present a continual procession of images that was not available to premodern society. Nature provided most of the images in premodern cultures. The design of man-made objects followed natural principles of practical necessity and aesthetic beauty. They were not designed to communicate something, except those images produced for ecclesiastical use and the accoutrements of the wealthy, intended to display social status.

It is increasingly difficult to communicate only using words. Much of the money spent by businesses on computer software and hardware is not for the processing of information, but for improving its visual display. Color monitors, sophisticated graphics programs, desktop publishing, and presentation graphics generators are all used to communicate visually. You can't just tell someone something, you have to *show* them. Television is a big part of the corporate world.

Over 8,000 U.S. businesses now operate their own TV networks. "Most of our employees are used to getting information off the job from television," says a manager at Pacific Bell. "So, we're seeing it as a natural way of communicating inside the company." "They'll watch anything," says the training director at Tab Products, Inc. "They are conditioned to TV."[6]

But would they *read* anything? Not likely.

PICTURE THIS

Images are a means of communicating knowledge, just as words are, but they are two different kinds of knowledge. Images communicate immediately and intuitively. Images are scanned in a subjective pattern. They are a splendid form to use to communicate concrete quantitative information or narratives.

Words, on the other hand, communicate through abstraction and analysis. Words communicate in linear, logical form; something communicated in words can thus be judged to be true or false. But an image cannot be true or false. This has led some media theorists, such as Tony Schwartz, to declare that truth is an outdated concept, belonging to an age dominated by print rather than television.[7]

Images can present a story, but not an argument. They can establish a mood, but they are incapable of articulating even the most simple distinctions of language. For example, here are seven simple sentences:

1) The cat is on the mat.
2) The cat is not on the mat.
3) The cat was on the mat.
4) The cat likes to be on the mat.
5) The cat should not be on the mat.
6) Get off the mat, cat!
7) If the cat doesn't get off the mat, I shall kick it.

Of these sentences, only the first could be presented visually, and then only with some uncertainty. I could show you a picture of a cat on a mat. But you might not even notice the mat. Depending on how interesting the cat was, if I asked you to give me a verbal equivalent of that image, you might say, "A cat," or "A brown cat," or "A pretty brown cat reclining and about ready to go to sleep." The mat may not attract any attention at all. But the verb in the sentence "The cat is on the mat" is also missing from the three imaginary responses. The simplest act of predication, linking a noun to a verb in a direct, unequivocal fashion, is uncertain with images.

Now try to imagine a picture that unambiguously communicated the second sentence. Would you show a cat next to a mat? That wouldn't necessarily communicate the relation that we're interested in, that of the cat not being on the mat. It might be interpreted as "A cat next to a mat." Would you show two pictures in succession, one with a cat on a mat and the next with a cat not on the mat? Perhaps, but you would most likely "read" that as, "The cat moved off the mat." Any idea of motion is much easier to communicate in pictures (especially in moving pictures) than any idea of *being*. The simplest verb in all human language, to be, is the hardest to present visually. Yet it is the verb that God used to define Himself as the great I AM.

We had a problem with simple predication and with negation. Communicating the past tense through an image or a series of images is also difficult. The same sequence of pictures we imagined for the second sentence, a picture of a cat on a mat and a cat not on a mat, could equally serve for "The cat was on the mat."

Trying to communicate that the cat likes to be on the mat takes us to another level of expression. Partly because cats seem so inscrutable, this one might be impossible. If we can't express without ambiguity the simple fact of the cat's being on the mat, it is even more difficult to communicate that the cat likes it there.

Finally, images are wholly inadequate to express what ought to be, what ought not to be, or conditions under which something will or will not happen. In images, everything is in the present tense and the indicative mood. Images are very nonjudgmental and undemanding. This poses some obvious problems for theology and ethics.

It also poses problems for the culture at large. It might be that one of the reasons there is so little in the way of shared norms in our society is that our shared mode of knowledge, television, works *against* the communication of norms. A culture that is rooted more in images than in words will find it increasingly difficult to sustain any broad commitment to *any* truth, since truth is an abstraction requiring language.

Words offer commands and prohibitions. Images establish feelings of resonance. Images remind us of things. They involve recognition more than cognition. Tony Schwartz argues that television strikes a "responsive chord" in us, that it works best when it resonates with something already in us.

> The critical task [for media producers, whether entertainers, advertisers, or educators] is to design our package of stimuli [i.e., programming] so that it resonates with information already stored witin an individual and thereby induces the desired learning or behavioral effect. Resonance takes place when the stimuli put into our communication evoke meaning in a listener or viewer. That which we put into the communication has no meaning in itself.[8]

This description by Schwartz fits perfectly with our description of the aesthetics of popular culture listed in Chapter Six.

Television discourages reflection, tells us what we already know, relies on instant accessibility, reminds us of something else, and reflects the desires of the self. It is the perfect medium for popular culture. As our culture became more dominated by images, and television increased in influence, it was almost technically inevitable that the shallow aesthetics of popular culture would eclipse the more reflective, deliberate aesthetic of high culture. High culture is not all expressed in print, but it requires the disciplines of a print-based society to be sustained.

SEEING AND BELIEVING

Before going on to discuss other attributes of television, we need to look at an earlier debate about the propriety of image-based culture. At the time of the Reformation, there was a controversy over images in the churches. The Protestant iconoclasts, those who destroyed statuary and other religious art, are today regarded as fanatical philistines. Without condoning all that they did, it may be helpful to consider some of the rationale for their vigorous antipathy to images.

The principal Biblical argument for iconoclasm was the prohibition in the Ten Commandments against graven images. Jacques Ellul notes that the painters, sculptors, and architects whose works were destroyed may certainly have worked "with all their faith, consecration, and service, in order to praise and glorify God." They were both marvelous artists and dedicated Christians. But, Ellul argues, there were church leaders and theologians who were inclined to make the church's presence in the world more visible, in the interest of efficiency of communication. The purpose of the proliferation of images in churches (which accelerated rapidly in the fourteenth century) was to attract the interest of illiterate peasants toward the gospel. The images were, in a sense, the church-controlled mass media of the day. Ellul quotes Charles Dumoulin, who wrote that "it is easier to look at paintings than to understand doctrine."9

But there was a price for that ease of communication, just as there is a price today for the ease of images over words. Images and seeing began to assume a central place in both piety and theology. Mystical theology, which emphasized inward vision, began to supplant systematic theology. "The ideal is to contemplate God himself. In order to do so, one must begin by contemplating pious images."[10] As a result of these changes,

> the word is repressed. It doesn't matter whether anyone understands what is said. What matters is to see what is done, and thus to participate physically. . . . It is much less important to live one's faith than to mime it, participating with one's body. Knowing revealed truth matters less than being involved in a corporeal imitation of it. For some, gesture is the main thing; for others, seeing replaces everything. The body occupies a position of considerable importance through a sort of contagion.[11]

Ellul makes the connection between medieval Christian piety and the effort of modern artists and scholars to recover a more intuitive, more physical, less rational form of knowing.

> When I hear serious scholarly presentations of the pedagogical role of images, I remember that all this was *precisely* stated by clerics and friars in the fourteenth century. I often think about the utterly convinced, impassioned look of those who talk about the new theater and its unheard-of discovery of direct participation, in which the spectator enters into the act; and the pride of the specialists and young people who rediscover the body (struggling against this abominable Christianity that has covered over, restrained, and eliminated the body) and tell us pompously about corporeal expression, which will replace useless spoken language. It is through the body, mime, and the contagion based on visual stimulation that one transmits . . . what? No, we no longer transmit anything. We only participate. Just listen to all these innovative, revolutionary statements, these discoveries of things never before known in the West (since, of course, the peoples of the Third World have retained the authenticity of corporeal expression, spontaneous theater and ceremony, carnivals and bodily participation in the Mass). When I hear all this, I sud-

denly find myself right back in the fourteenth century, when all this talk — exactly the same thing — was already being heard, and from Christians![12]

Tony Schwartz and Jacques Ellul seem to agree on the essential differences between print-based and image-based cultures. They only disagree on their evaluation of it. If Ellul sounds too hysterical, consider Schwartz's recommendations to educators about overcoming the bias of print in teaching basic skills.

> *Concentration* . . . is a valuable skill in reading but unimportant in electronic learning. . . . In reading, the ability to learn depends on the ability to concentrate. With electronic media it is *openness* that counts. . . . Moreover, someone who is taught to concentrate will fail to perceive many patterns of information conveyed by electronic stimuli.[13]

In case there is still any doubt, the next paragraph should make it clear that Mr. Schwartz will not be offered a job as a consultant for the Barbara Bush Foundation for Family Literacy, although he is no doubt a great fan of "Channel One."

> A child does not have to read in order to acquire knowledge. This is not to argue that reading is an unimportant skill. However, it is no longer an essential skill that must be acquired before a child can grow up intellectually. Schools might well adopt a task-orientation approach to reading skills. A child should learn to read when he needs to read, or when he wants to take a "literacy trip." With a task-orientation approach, the age at which a child learns to read may change. Reading will not be the first task a child encounters when he enters school. Also, he will learn to read material that relates to his life. One teacher in New Jersey applied this principle and achieved remarkable success in teaching high school dropouts to read. Instead of using elementary reading textbooks, he employed pornographic literature as source material. He was fired.[14]

Schwartz's position seems to be an extreme one, but one wonders how many "leading educators" agree with him, whether or not they will admit it. One of the principal reasons for being literate is to be able to distinguish truth from falsehood. But if that distinction is regarded as less and less important in our lives, in politics, in art, in relationships, in religion, than why bother learning to read?

ONCE UPON A TIME

Most of the time a television is turned on, it is expected to entertain. Even news programs must be entertaining. Television communicates and entertains using three main forms: it tells stories, it depicts conversations, and it displays action. All three of these forms are *dramatic* forms, which has led critic Martin Esslin to suggest that "the language of television is none other than that of *drama*." [15] Esslin says that drama is not only a language, but a "method of thinking, of experiencing the world and reasoning about it."[16]

Esslin points out that even the news uses these dramatic forms. Journalists in all media refer to the reports they do as "stories," and in television more than any other form, that is more than a metaphor. Since many topics covered by journalists are naturally complex and abstract, and since television's visual bias prefers simplicity and concreteness, the story is an easy way to present the news, especially since you might have to explain something like the latest eruption of violence in Beirut in about ninety seconds.

The solution television offers is to find a cast of characters and a narrative line. Even if the story is intrinsically abstract, such as a rise in unemployment, a reporter is best-advised to find an unemployed person and tell his or her story. The story-form introduces certain predictable biases in television news, but that is not our concern here. What may be more significant is that the form of the story obscures analysis of the content of the news, even as it furthers the idea that anything worth knowing about can be presented in a lively way. Docudramas and infotainment are not alien to TV news. They are natural developments of TV's need to entertain.

There are news-conversation shows as well. These are often more informative than the nightly newscasts, especially in the hands of a vigorous conversationalist. The word is more respected in this setting than in any other place on television. Unfortunately, most of these programs are programmed in low viewing slots (Sunday morning, early afternoon, and *Nightline* after prime time is well over), and the people who watch them tend to be more print-oriented than most, people who are regular readers, at least of newspapers and newsmagazines. Such programs do not have much of an effect on encouraging analytical skills in the population at large. These programs are not less entertaining, if done well, than other shows, although a small proportion of the audience may find them so.

There is nothing wrong with wanting to be entertained. But television's role as an entertainment appliance presents at least two problems. The first is that access to entertainment is so easy. Regular television viewers expect to be entertained regularly. Entertainment is the one constant in their lives. "Entertainment Tonight" is a demand, not a possibility. Such a state of mind is surely unhealthy, especially when, as for Montaigne, the addiction to diversion serves to prevent reflection on one's eternal destiny.

In the introduction to his thoughtful book *Amusing Ourselves to Death: Public Discourse in an Age of Show Business*, Neil Postman explains that the purpose of his book, published in 1985, was to reflect, not on Orwell's chilling prophecy for the previous year, but on the slightly earlier vision of Aldous Huxley's *Brave New World*, whose account of dystopia is not as well-known in our day, perhaps because it is more critical of the media than of government.

What Orwell feared were those who would ban books. What Huxley feared was that there would be no reason to ban a book, for there would be no one who wanted to read one. Orwell feared those who would deprive us of information. Huxley feared those who would give us so much that we would be reduced to passivity and egoism. Orwell feared that the truth would be concealed from us. Huxley feared the truth would be drowned in a sea of irrelevance. Orwell feared we would become a captive culture. Huxley feared we would become a trivial culture, preoccupied with some equivalent of the feelies, the orgy porgy, and the centrifugal bumblepuppy. As Huxley remarked in *Brave New World Revisited*, the civil libertarians and rationalists who are ever on the alert to oppose tyranny "failed to take into account man's almost infinite appetite for distraction." In *1984*, Huxley added, people are controlled by inflicting pain. In *Brave New World*, they are controlled by inflicting pleasure. In short, Orwell feared that what we hate will ruin us. Huxley feared that what we love will ruin us.[17]

The second problem with television is related to the nature of the medium as *visual* and *dramatic*. As Martin Esslin has pointed out, these two qualities are very much related, since "in drama the complex, multilayered image predominates over the spoken word."[18] The dramatic images of television have much more power than anything that is *said* on the air; television doesn't have much time for encouraging reflection. It is the perfect popular culture medium, for, even at its best, it is a means of promoting the immediate experience as the dominant way of dealing with life. Reflection, analysis, and reasonable discrimination are discouraged. Esslin argues that in dramatic communication, the "linguistic element, insofar as it is concerned with the transmission of abstract ideas, may often come very far down our ladder, after gesture and movement, after costume, even after the impact of setting."[19] Abstract ideas are, however, essential to the maintenance of the social order; freedom, justice, and duty, to name a few abtractions, can be *illustrated* in drama, but understanding the essence of them requires the analytic powers of language.

More significantly, Christian obedience requires at least some familiarity with certain abstractions, such as sin, forgiveness, love, holiness, and eternity. Once again, such abstractions can be demonstrated in narrative or dramatic form, but drama is no better than images at communicating the essence of what God has revealed in propositions.

Even if all of the entertainment on television was inoffen-
sive to Christian ethics and of the highest artistic merit, its form
of communication (and form of knowing) encourages the aver-
sion to abstraction, analysis, and reflection that characterizes our
culture at all levels. Thinking is often hard work. Television's sur-
feit of instant entertainment not only provides relief from such
hard work; it offers an attractive, alternative "way of knowing"
(as does rock 'n' roll) that makes reasoning seem anachronistic,
narrow, and unnecessary.

USER FRIENDLY

We love television not only because it entertains, but because we
love (or love to hate) the characters it portrays, whether Peter
Jennings, the Equalizer, or Alf. Like his peers Dan and Tom
(never Daniel or Thomas) Peter Jennings is, after all, playing a
role as much as any other television actor. He is playing the role
of Peter Jennings, anchorman. He is avuncular, wise, and friend-
ly. TV news on the morning programs goes one step better: it
doesn't just have reporters, it has *hosts*. What a warm, hospitable gesture, to be hosts to us, to take us into their home (even
if it only is a set of a home) while telling us stories about various
distant atrocities and reminding us to take an umbrella.

The illusion of intimacy which television presents is sometimes breathtaking. Pat Robertson looks into the camera and
prays for *me*. Bruce Willis looks into the camera and winks at
me. We share a space of mutual understanding (and flattery) that
is unachievable in any other medium, except perhaps that rare
form called "real life." But TV can seem to be even more intimate than face-to-face encounters, which always involve more
vulnerability, require more patience, and threaten more disap-
pointment. The worst thing a television friend can do to us is get
canceled, but we really shouldn't take that personally.

Even as television seems to create a shared space of intimacy, it destroys other important social relations. In his study *No
Sense of Place: The Impact of Electronic Media on Social
Behavior*,[20] Joshua Meyrowitz argues that television erodes our
sense of important social distances. It blurs the difference

between the public and the private sphere. One of the most remarkable things about programs such as those hosted by Phil Donahue or Oprah Winfrey is the degree of intimate detail people are willing to reveal about themselves in front of a camera. Perhaps it is because they are used to consuming such detail in front of their sets. People will (both literally and figuratively) expose themselves for a television audience.[21]

Television's illusion of intimacy is another way in which popular culture makes a promise of immediacy. Everyone is on a first-name basis, everyone can share everything, no one has any authority. Not only is there (in Daniel Bell's term) an eclipse of distance between the individual and experience, there is an eclipse of distance between all individuals and all experiences. As television uses satellites and portable cameras to ignore the concept of *literal* space, it also does away with the idea of social or moral place, the idea that some behavior is appropriate to some settings and inappropriate to others. Television erases the very idea of propriety. Thus, the production of programs some people find morally offensive is entirely in keeping with the nature of the medium.

While television distorts our sense of the significance of literal and social space, it also distorts our sense of time, thereby assisting other forms of popular culture in the effort to make the past and the future avoidable. The ability to record an event (or, more accurately, the visual impressions of an event) is something we take for granted, but it is surely as significant a cultural development as the introduction of movable type. The proliferation of VCRs, which gives television viewers much more control over television (which is a good thing), also futher distorts our experience of time (which is not a good thing). The act of recording a program to watch it later is called "time shifting" by people who work in the medium. It wreaks havoc on their effort to sell commercial "time." But it has other effects as well. As TV critic Tom Shales points out,

> We are all time shifters now. Or time shiftees. Time is for shifting. In an electronic society, where every day is a Broadcast Day, time takes on a new relativity, relatively

speaking. We're afloat in an illusory symbol world; we're not lost out here in the stars but out here in the electrons. Television, where it's always now, is almost always some other time as well. What does it do to us? You might say it gives us jet lag all the time. Or at least time lag all the time.[22]

Shales suggests that the habit of watching reruns, whether supplied by the networks, by cable, or by our own VCR, fits quite nicely with the lack of a sense of time that characterized the 1980s. The eighties, which Shales dubs the "Re Decade," had "no texture, no style and tone of their own." Instead they had "the texture and style and tone of all the other decades, at least those that were recorded on film or tape."[23] Of course, reruns of "The Honeymooners" or "Leave It to Beaver" are now received with a knowing sense of superiority; like much of our culture, they are perceived with an ironic detachment, a sensibility that critics label postmodern. This mood of irony, often lapsing into cynicism, detectable in all reaches of popular culture, is the perfect mood for television. As Shales observes:

> Television *is* the culture, of course. What it does and what it fixates on affects everything else. Values are being reordered, like the value of timeliness, which is itself becoming passé. The Re Decade makes a mockery of a lot of things. What it may most make a mockery of is this phrase: "The fullness of time." It feels like the emptiness of time now.[24]

GUMBY, COME HOME

Part of that emptiness is due to the growing sense in our culture that, as Umberto Eco has observed, we cannot cut off the past entirely, but neither can we revisit it innocently. Having lived through The Sixties, today's television watchers cannot go back to The Fifties as innocents: that would be to deny that The Sixties had any meaning. But they want to go back. So they return wearing the armor of irony. A favorite show of this generation, "thirtysomething," is filled with this sort of ironic nostalgia. David Letterman's humor thrives on it. So does that of Steve Martin, John Candy, and Chevy Chase. What is surprising is that Pee-Wee Herman's does too. Parents watch Pee-Wee Herman as a postmodernist cross between Jerry Lewis and Howdy Doody. It's funny because it's so *knowing*, like having a Gumby on your desk, putting pink flamingos on your lawn, or wearing a double-knit leisure suit to a party.

Umberto Eco describes the postmodernist mood this way:

> I think of the postmodern attitude as that of a man who loves a very cultivated woman and knows he cannot say to her, "I love you madly," because he knows that she knows (and that she knows that he knows) that these words have already been written by Barbara Cartland. Still, there is a solution. He can say, "As Barbara Cartland would put it, I love you madly." At this point, having avoided false innocence, having said clearly that it is no longer possible to speak innocently, he will nevertheless have said what he wanted to say to the woman: that he loves her, but he loves her in an age of lost innocence. If the woman goes along with this, she will have received a declaration of love all the same. Neither of the two speakers will feel innocent, both will have accepted the challenge of the past, of the already said, which cannot be eliminated; both will consciously and with pleasure play the game of irony. . . . But both will have succeeded, once again, in speaking of love.[25]

But is it really saying the same thing as once could be said? Could it be that the postmodernist mood, which many say is the only available mood of our times, and which is certainly most pronounced in popular culture, makes sincerity and guilessness impossible? I do not know. I do believe that addiction to television (as opposed to deliberate, measured viewing) makes sincere and deep relationships with people and with reality more difficult to sustain. Tom Shales, a great lover of television, nonethless is concerned that media-mediated reality can become very *un*real.

When an attempt was made on President Reagan's life during his first term, the act was caught on tape, and the image was replayed and replayed until it became virtually meaningless, as meaningless as a deodorant commercial or a line-drive base hit from last July or the hottest music video of the first week in the third month of 1984. Could time be one of those things in which humanity was not meant to meddle?[26]

BONDAGE OF CHOICE

In 1987, NBC-TV ran a series of ads promoting its network by telling viewers how wonderful television was. Each of the ads featured a prominent figure musing (supposedly impromptu) about the great achievement of television in making our lives better. Dr. Benjamin Spock ("Pediatrician. Author. Peace Activist") appeared in one of the more stupid of the spots. He essentially said that television was good because kids could have fun watching it and it was cheaper than the movies ("It's right there in the living room"). Fade to black. Superimpose tag line: "NBC: Tuning into America." Of course, NBC was *really* worried about whether or not America was tuned into *it*.

The previous year ABC-TV had run a similar series, but it was more in the form of "info-merical." Jim Duffy, president of communications of ABC, appeared in each of the spots giving us some information about the television business, the world behind the screen, and tried to help us see the big picture, as it were. These campaigns seem to have the competition from cable and videotapes in view as much as the other networks. One of Duffy's spots ended with this quasi-philosophical appeal: "Nobody could watch it all," he informed us. "And that's the point. There *is* a *choice. Your* choice. American television and you."

Both of these spots made reference to America, perhaps because, as Mark Crispin Miller has suggested, both television and America promise the same thing: choice. In America, citizens

are not ground down by party rule, church dictate, authoritarian tyranny, or the daily dangers of fanatical vendetta; and in this atmosphere of peace and plenty, they are free to work and play, have families, and contemplate, if not yet actually enjoy, the bounty of our unprecedented system.[27]

Miller quotes Clint Suggs, who in 1985 had been one of the hostages held by Shiite gunmen aboard TWA Flight 847 in Lebanon. After returning home, Suggs talked in an interview about the freedom available in America, and how being in captivity made him appreciate it so much more. "When we sit here in our living room, with the sun setting, the baby sleeping, we can watch television, change channels. We have choices."[28]

Well, one has to hope that the Founders had a bit more in mind when they were working on the Constitution, but, yes, you can change channels. In fact, thanks to remote control, changing channels is kind of fun. Jumping from one program to another and then to another is almost like art. At least like *some* art.

Robert Hughes has noted that the "swift montage and juxtaposition" of images that characterizes TV viewing has had an effect on the modern consciousness. The effect has been, he maintains, "to insulate and estrange us from reality itself, turning everything into disposable spectacle: catastrophe, love, war, soap. Ours is the cult of the electronic fragment."[29] Nobody could watch it all. But even in watching those fragments, the nature of the choosing is transformed. The fundamental assumption of the world of television, argues Neil Postman, is not coherence but discontinuity.[30] Choosing in a coherent world requires deliberation and thoughtfulness, but choosing in the midst of chaos becomes arbitrary, a sheer act of will.

In 1985 Pepsi began a series of ads the theme of which was, "Pepsi: The Choice of a New Generation." Many of them (for Pepsi and Diet Pepsi) were understated and spare, with no catchy jingles to ornament the slogan, no moonwalking to fire the senses. The dramatic setting of the ads usually involved a pair of close friends, lovers, or relatives talking playfully about some personal matter, occasionally taking a swig from a can of Pepsi. All of the spots were shot in a voyeuristic series of close-ups, a hand-held camera giving us fragments of detail, but little sense of context (just like TV itself). These were keyhole images of intimacy without place, isolated vignettes of the new generation making choices.

The most disturbing ad featured Geraldine Ferraro, who along with Walter Mondale had just lost the election. In the ad with her were her two daughters, and the conversation was about choosing careers. Two-thirds of the way into the commercial, the announcer for the whole series of ads, Martin Sheen, declared, "When you make a choice, what's right is what *feels* right." Then Ms. Ferraro said to one daughter, "You know, there's one choice I'll never regret." The daughter queries, "Being a politician?" Slight pause, then Ms. Ferraro corrects her gently: "Being a mother."

There was a lot more going on here than selling soda pop. Here was a spot that was pro-family *and* pro-choice. It affirmed moral relativism while charming us with a glimpse of a mother and daughters sharing some quality time. To associate the word "choice" with Ms. Ferraro, especially in the context of choosing to be a mother, was more chilling than a cold Pepsi. After all, the issue of "choice" had dogged Ms. Ferarro throughout the campaign. She had made it clear that she was "personally opposed" to the choice millions of women make *not* to be a mother after the mechanism of maternity had already been engaged. But she had also insisted that the right to choose abortion was at the foundation of women's rights in America (after all, what's right is what *feels* right, right?).

The choice of the new generation, the television generation (comin' at you, goin' strong), is untrammeled choice. It is in the interest of television to perpetuate its gospel of choice. After all, it makes us feel good to have choices. But it is not in the interest of television to have us think too hard about our choices, either our choices about what to watch, what to buy, or how to live. The development of reflective habits might mean that we choose not to watch television as often as we do now. Television's place of supremacy in society depends on the fact that we often turn it on and keep it on without really deliberately choosing to do so, any more than we choose to turn on the lights when we enter a dark room, or choose every half hour to keep them on. Nobody could watch it all, but we'll sure try.

WHERE DO WE GO FROM HERE?

"Negativism! . . . Everything you have said is negative. . . . What positive proposals do you have and what program do you suggest?" So Jacques Ellul anticipated the response to his book *The Humiliation of the Word.*[1] I think I can safely assume that some readers of this book will feel the same way. Ellul compared his book with the freeing of a prisoner from chains. His analysis of the "humiliation of the word" described the bondage to images that characterized the culture and the church. By identifying the bondage, he provided a means of escape. But liberation is a negative work: destroying chains involves the destruction of the work of someone else as well as the choices of others. Mere liberation presents no program or agenda for action. It simply sets a person free.

Ellul concluded that "the only positive action we can take is to open a space into which we must dash forward."[2] But I think we can do more than that. We can suggest *how* one might dash and *toward what*.

Many Christians are interested in the answer to the question, "How can I enjoy popular culture in a way that is consistent with a Christian worldview?" What if someone were to ask, "How can I enjoy sexuality in a way that is consistent with a Christian worldview?" It would not be responsible to answer simply by offering a catalogue of sexual behavior and saying, "These are things you can do, and these are things you can't." Rather, we should start by understanding sexuality in the context in which God created it, by examining its significance in light of other activities and responsibilities and relationships. A good answer would begin with a question, "What is the nature of human sexuality?"

Of course, such an answer may not satisfy the impatient adolescent who simply wants to know "how far" he can go without sinning. But the cultivation of a Christian worldview is not a matter of defining the "bottom line." It involves reflecting on the nature of things, on the place they have in the larger scheme of creation and redemption, in human nature and in history.

Unlike human sexuality, popular culture is not something created by God. But neither was the meat offered to the Corinthian idols. The issue at hand in 1 Corinthians 10 was whether or not meat that had been associated with the cultural trappings of idolatry could be consumed. Paul's answer was to appeal to a text about creation: "The earth is the Lord's, and everything in it." In the context of Psalm 24, this is a verse about creation in its pristine state, not the mangled, sin-corrupted work of man. But Paul believed that the cultural context in which the meat existed was irrelevant *to those believers who were dead to that idolatrous culture.*

My answer to the question about Christian involvement with popular culture is essentially the same. You can enjoy popular culture without compromising Biblical principles *as long as you are not dominated by the sensibility of popular culture, as long as you are not captivated by its idols.*

A LONG AND WINDING ROAD

This book has been an effort to explain the nature of popular culture in relation to other aspects of creation, and especially in relation to the history of American culture and society. Escaping the captivity to popular culture's ethos requires that we know how that ethos differs from other cultural alternatives, and how it has evolved to reflect other ideas in our culture.

We have come a long way in examining that evolution. We looked at how popular culture emerged in the nineteenth century as a substitute for traditional or folk culture, for people uprooted from those cultures by industrialism. We saw how popular culture's mass-produced, disposable quality established limits to what it could contain, even as they encouraged greater and greater consumption. We saw how, in the twentieth century, popular culture effectively preempted the place of high culture, as the values of high culture, a legacy of Romanticism, became indistinguishable from those of popular culture. We examined the crucial decade of the 1960s, in which the superficial, antirational, and immediate qualities of popular culture were more and more regarded not merely as a means of distraction, but as a means of intense and liberating knowledge of the universe.

As we approach the twenty-first century, popular culture is taking the lead in establishing a sensibility, not of intense involvement, but of cool detachment. Its view of the past and the future is no less fractured, and its sentimentality remains.

While each of these transformations follows a certain logic, none of them has been predictable. We cannot imagine what sensibility the popular culture of the coming decades will encourage. But we must be on our guard. It may have been easier for the Corinthians to eat meat offered to idols than it is for us to enjoy popular culture innocently. Idolatry is so obviously foreign to Christian values that it is must be guarded against constantly. Even idolatrous ideas are not too difficult to identify and resist. But a sensibility, a consciousness, is much more evasive and subtle.

This book could have been a lot more relaxed (and perhaps a lot more fun) if the church in America was as alert to the problems of the sensibility of popular culture as the church in Corinth was to the significance of idol worship. But instead, while critical of some of its content, the church has a virtually uncritical attitude toward the form of popular culture. In fact, the church has adopted those forms without much resistance, in the alleged interest of promoting its message. But the message has thereby suffered, and so have its members. A Christianity presented as a "natural high," as a "rewarding lifestyle option," or as "the key to health and wealth" is not the faith once delivered to the saints. Our God is too small because our culture is too small. Popular culture's forms are not capable of sustaining the Christian conviction of a holy, judging God who demands repentance and promises the joy of obedience.

Ellul argued that the church of the fourteenth century saw the promotion of image-oriented devotion as an *effective* way of promoting the work of the gospel. Well before the advent of modernity, it seems, *efficiency* had captured the church's imagination. But having accepted images as a practical means of communication, the church modified its theology by "contextualizing" its teaching to accommodate the proliferation of images. The requirements of efficiency dictated the dominance of a new medium, and the medium changed the message. The church rearranged its doctrine from an emphasis on the word to an emphasis on the image.

As in the fourteenth century, the twentieth-century church seems to value efficiency over the integrity of its message. The fourteenth century left in its wake numerous heresies and superstitions, and required the radical break of the Reformation to reestablish a sensibility that was not hostile to the truth. The twentieth century sees churches competing with popular culture *on its own terms*, "on the basis of their ability to titillate the instincts of their worshippers," turning the shepherds of the sheep into "entrepreneurs of emotional stimulation."[3]

I am not suggesting that we become twentieth-century iconoclasts, smashing television sets and boom boxes. I am suggesting that Christians could provide leadership in encouraging cultural habits that go against the grain of the search for immediate fulfillment.

A LOST OPPORTUNITY

In the two decades since the cultural collapse provoked by The Sixties, there have been numerous laments from a cultural remnant about the loss of a sense of transcendence, absolutes, and human dignity. Many intellectuals are chafing under the yoke of oppression from ideologies that see all cultural expressions as political, expressive only of interests of class, race, and gender. What a shame that these intellectuals (many of them agnostic or atheistic) could not look at the church and see *in its cultural expressions as well as in its teaching a living testimony to a culture of transcendence*, a dynamic cultural life rooted in permanent things.

The call to escape the bondage to the sensibility of popular culture is not a call to asceticism. It is an invitation to expect *more* from our cultural lives, not less — at least more that is true, noble, right, pure, lovely, and admirable. Having resisted the idolatry encouraged by popular culture (the self-centered obsession with the new, the immediate, the sensuous, and the spectacular), we can enjoy *all* cultural activities more fully, at least those capable of being enjoyed. Books, plays, films, painting, television, music, and sports can all be better appreciated once we approach them as we ought. Of course, we may find that some of the more popular songs or television programs or books are really not capable of being enjoyed; their only power may be to titillate and distract. But we have not lost anything thereby, except perhaps the possibility of being fashionably in tune with what's hot. I can remember in junior high school (a time when being fashionable is of immense importance) worrying that I might grow out of liking certain popular music. At the time it seemed the height of bliss, and I resisted any aesthetic progress that took me away from what I *knew* I liked and didn't want ever not to like.

There have been other books that give very practical advice about "what you can do about T.V., movies, books and music."[4] This book has been marked by a much more theoretical concern, but I hope that it will have great practical significance for those who heed its observations.

PARENTING FOR TRUTH AND BEAUTY

Parents have a great obligation to establish a cultural sensibility in their children. I think that children whose home life is characterized by a culture of transcendence will have a great advantage in resisting the temptations of popular culture in later years.

Television is perhaps the biggest problem. It is, after all, a wonderful plug-in drug.[5] What mother or father doesn't welcome the moments of relative peace and quiet when toddlers are narcotized by TV? But TV not only induces addiction to itself: it induces addiction to the sensibility of popular culture — the quest for novel, distracting, and easy entertainment. It is a great challenge for parents to substitute imaginative reading, music, storytelling, drama, drawing, and crafts for the ready-made fun of TV, but this is certainly a worthy investment. Parents should be eager to instill in their children the idea that enjoying cultural activity usually takes some work, but that the results are much more rewarding than those offered by instant entertainment.

I don't think total abstinence from TV is necessary or wise. Thanks to videocassette recorders, it is much easier today for parents to control what their children watch than it was in the past. There are many pre-recorded tapes available that avoid the frenetic pace and mindless narrative of most Saturday morning fare. They would be worth purchasing (perhaps in a parents co-op, so a number of families could pool resources and build up a collective library).

Commercials are the most disturbing aspect of children's television, not so much because they induce coveteousness or greed, but because they are so visually and aurally complex. Most commercials produced for kids have an aesthetic quality that is extremely deadening. They are the visual and aural equivalent of stuffing kids' mouths full of potato chips and soda, and then rewarding the one who eats it all the fastest. The sensibility of children's television commercials is generally one of immediate, vivid, and irrational gratification. If they do in fact work very well at persuading kids to badger their parents into buying things for them, they are also the perfect form for encouraging the worst aspects of popular culture's consciousness.

TEACH OUR CHILDREN WELL

I do not envy the teachers of America. Everyone tells them how they should be doing their jobs. I have no desire to add to the chorus (at least not in *this* book), but since they have a great influence on inculcating our children with their cultural values, I will offer a few observations.

Christian teachers should give more thought to what their teaching *methods* communicate. Methods should not be evaluated simply in terms of a narrow range of goals. If media are messages, then *how* one teaches is as significant as *what* one teaches. Eduators need to ask whether the critical reasoning skills they want to groom in their students are really served by the plethora of image-based educational materials, especially on television.

Students are not merely acquiring facts in school. They are acquiring a cultural sensibility. Of course, the culture of their peers (usually dominated by popular culture) is the most compelling form presented to them. But teachers can have a profound effect by offering their students a glimpse of cultural options that provide opportunities for much richer experience.

IF YOU CAN'T TEACH, DO

Those who produce popular culture have some peculiar challenges. Obviously, Christians who believe they are called to work in popular culture need to be certain they are not suffering from its debilitating effects. They also ought to find ways of communicating to their public that there is more to life than seeking entertainment. The "There's No Business Like Show Business" gospel makes for wonderful publicity, but it can obscure the limitations of popular culture.

Those working in narrative forms, such as television drama or popular fiction, have some special opportunities. An episode of a police drama that focuses on questions of integrity, duty, courage, and justice is better than a show which features nothing more than a series of car chases. Focusing on such questions is also better than moralizing about some fashionable current social issue. One of the reasons for the emptiness of even some of the best television and film is the tendency for writers, directors, and producers to strive for depth by dealing with a current social or political problem. But social problems, however severe, are still ephemeral, and unless the script escapes the bumper-sticker level and deals with the timeless human problems suggested by these social ills, it can easily be an exercise in trendiness.

FAITHFUL SHEPHERDS

Finally, church leaders have some particular opportunities. They need to ask to what extent the cultural sensibilities associated with the church reflect the objective concerns of Christian truth, and to what extent they reflect the subjective standards of the spirit of the age. Those Christians within the evangelical tradition have some special challenges because of evangelicalism's loose definition. Some historians and sociologists have identified evangelicalism as a community of *orthodoxy*, of concern for right belief. But there are so many doctrines on which self-proclaimed evangelicals disagree that one must ask whether or not contemporary evangelicalism is better defined as a community of *orthopathos*, of concern for right feeling. We disagree on the nature and extent of salvation, on the meaning of the Sacraments, on the nature of revelation (both general and special), on the nature of church authority and structure, on the work of the Holy Spirit, and on eschatology. But when evangelicals gather, they tend to enjoy singing the same sorts of hymns, they tend to use similar means of expression for talking about their faith, and they tend to express very similar sentiments not only about their faith, but about other matters as well.

In short, evangelicals seem to have more in common concerning the sentimental trappings associated with faith than they do in defining what the nature of that faith is. This is not just saying that they have all *experienced* the same faith, for I believe that many nonevangelicals have also experienced the same faith. But what distinguishes evangelicalism as a subculture or movement is a certain *feeling* about faith.

If the movement known as evangelicalism promotes a culture of sentiment rather than a culture of reasoned reflection, it is not surprising that popular culture has been as dominant (if not quite as vulgar) within evangelical circles as in the society at large.

The challenge for evangelical leaders is to be able to stand back and ask to what extent their movement and their churches have embraced certain cultural forms for the sake of expediency, just as the fourteenth-century church introduced a flood of image-based piety. These leaders need to become more sensitive to the way forms communicate values. This could lead to some radical changes, but so did the Reformation.

BIBLIOGRAPHY

Dore Ashton, *American Art Since 1945* (New York: Oxford University Press, 1982).

Paul Baker, *Contemporary Christian Music: Where It Came From, What It Is, Where It's Going* (Westchester, IL: Crossway Books, 1979).

Jacques Barzun, *Critical Questions: On Music and Letters, Culture and Biography, 1940-1980*, selected, edited, and introduced by Bea Friedland (Chicago: University of Chicago Press, 1982).

———, *Darwin, Marx, Wagner: Critique of a Heritage*, second edition (Garden City, NY: Anchor Books, 1958).

———, "Scholarship versus Culture," *The Atlantic*, November 1984, pp. 93-104.

Franklin L. Baumer, *Modern European Thought: Continuity and Change in Ideas, 1600-1950* (New York: Macmillan, 1977).

Daniel Bell, *The Coming of Post-Industrial Society: A Venture in Social Forecasting* (New York: Basic Books, 1973).

———, *The Cultural Contradictions of Capitalism* (New York: Basic Books, 1976, 1978).

Tony Bennett, Colin Mercer, Janet Woollacott, eds., *Popular Culture and Social Relations* (Philadelphia: Open University Press, 1986).

Laurence Bergreen, *Look Now, Pay Later: The Rise of Network Broadcasting* (Garden City, NY: Doubleday, 1980).

Marshall Berman, *All That Is Solid Melts into Air: The Experience of Modernity* (New York: Simon and Schuster, 1982).

K. L. Billingsley, *The Seductive Image: A Christian Critique of the World of Film (Westchester, IL: Crossway Books, 1989).*

Allan Bloom, *The Closing of the American Mind: How Higher Education Has Failed Democracy and Impoverished the Souls of Today's Students* (New York: Simon and Schuster, 1987).

Daniel Boorstin, *The Image, or What Happened to the American Dream?* (New York: Atheneum, 1962).

Malcolm Bradbury, James McFarlane, eds., *Modernism, 1890-1930* (New York: Penguin Books, 1976).

Pascal Bruckner, *The Tears of the White Man: Compassion as Contempt*, translated with an Introduction by William R. Beer (New York: The Free Press, 1986).

Paul Buhle, ed., *Popular Culture in America* (Minneapolis: University of Minnesota Press, 1987).

Matei Calinescu, *Faces of Modernity: Avant-garde, Decadence, Kitsch* (Bloomington, IN: Indiana University Press, 1977).

John G. Cawelti, "Review" of Jules Feiffer's *The Great Comic Book Heroes*, Marshall McLuhan's *The Medium Is the Message*, Tom Wolfe's *The Kandy-Kolored, Tangerine-Flake Streamline Baby*, and Susan Sontag's *Against Interpretation and Other Essays*, in *American Quarterly*, Summer 1968, pp. 254-259.

John Miller Chernoff, *African Rhythm and African Sensibility: Aesthetics and Social Action in African Musical Idioms* (Chicago: University of Chicago Press, 1979).

Kenneth Clark, *What Is a Masterpiece?* (New York: Thames and Hudson, 1979).

Ellen K. Coughlin, "In Face of Growing Success and Conservatives' Attacks, Cultural-Studies Scholars Ponder Future Directions," *Chronicle of Higher Education*, January 18, 1989, p. A-4f.

Frederick Crews, *Skeptical Engagements* (New York: Oxford University Press, 1986).

Douglas Davis, *Artculture: Essays on the Postmodern* (New York: Harper & Row, 1977).

Maureen Dowd, "Youth, Art, Hype: A Different Bohemia," *The New York Times Magazine*, November 17, 1985, pp. 26-42, 87ff.

Umberto Eco, *Postscript to the Name of the Rose*, translated from the Italian by William Weaver (San Diego: Harcourt Brace Jovanovich, 1984).

Thomas Stearns Eliot, *Christianity and Culture: The Idea of a Christian Society and Notes Towards the Definition of Culture* (New York: Harcourt Brace Jovanovich, 1968).

Jacques Ellul, *The Humiliation of the Word*, translated by Joyce Main Hanks (Grand Rapids, MI: Eerdmans, 1985).

———, *The Technological Society,.* translated from the French by John Wilkinson, with an Introduction by Robert K. Merton (New York: Alfred A. Knopf, 1964).

Joseph Epstein, "It's Only Culture," *Commentary*, November 1983, pp. 56-61.

Martin Esslin, *The Age of Television* (San Francisco: W. H. Freeman and Company, 1982).

Leslie Fiedler, *What Was Literature? Class Culture and Mass Society* (New York: Simon and Schuster, 1982).

Hal Foster, ed., *The Anti-Aesthetic: Essays on Postmodern Culture* (Port Townsend, WA: Bay Press, 1983).

Razelle Frankl, *Televangelism: The Marketing of Popular Religion* (Carbondale, IL: Southern Illinois University Press, 1987).

Simon Frith, Howard Horne, *Art into Pop* (New York: Methuen, 1987).

Simon Frith, ed., *Facing the Music* (New York: Pantheon Books, 1988).

———, *Music for Pleasure: Essays in the Sociology of Pop* (New York: Routledge, 1988).

Suzi Gablik, *Has Modernism Failed?* (London: Thames and Hudson, 1984).

Herbert J. Gans, *Popular Culture and High Culture: An Analysis and Evaluation of Taste* (New York: Basic Books, 1974).

John Gardner, *On Moral Fiction* (New York: Basic Books, 1978).

Ted Gioia, *The Imperfect Art: Reflections on Jazz and Modern Culture* (New York: Oxford University Press, 1988).

Todd Gitlin, "Hip-Deep in Post-modernism," *The New York Times Book Review*, November 6, 1988, pp. 1, 35ff.

———, ed., *Watching Television* (New York: Pantheon, 1986).

Gregor T. Goethals, *The TV Ritual: Worship at the Video Altar* (Boston: Beacon Press, 1981).

Carla Gottlieb, *Beyond Modern Art* (New York: E. P. Dutton, 1976).

Andrew M. Greeley, *God in Popular Culture* (Chicago: Thomas More Press, 1988).

Clement Greenberg, *Art and Culture: Critical Essays* (Boston: Beacon Press, 1961).

Bryan F. Griffin, *Panic Among the Philistines* (Chicago: Regnery Gateway, 1983).

Robert Harbison, *Deliberate Regression* (New York: Alfred A. Knopf, 1980).

Jeffrey Hart, *When the Going Was Good! American Life in the Fifties* (New York: Crown Publishers, 1982).

Rolf-Dieter Herrmann, "Art, Technology, and Nietzsche," *Journal of Aesthetics and Art Criticism*, Fall 1973, pp. 95-102.

George S. Heyer, Jr., *Signs of Our Times: Theological Essays on Art in the Twentieth Century* (Grand Rapids: Eerdmans, 1980).

Hal Himmelstein, *Television Myth and the American Mind* (New York: Praeger, 1984).

Robert Hughes, *The Shock of the New* (New York: Alfred A. Knopf, 1981).

James Davison Hunter, *American Evangelicalism: Conservative Religion and the Quandary of Modernity* (New Brunswick, NJ: Rutgers University Press, 1983).

Charles Jencks, *What Is Post-modernism?* (New York: St. Martin's Press, 1987).

Bertram Jessup, "Crisis in the Fine Arts Today," *The Journal of Aesthetics and Art Criticism*, Fall 1970, pp. 3-10.

Abraham Kaplan, "The Aesthetics of the Popular Arts," *The Journal of Aesthetics and Art Criticism*, Spring 1966, pp. 351-364.

E. Ann Kaplan, *Rocking Around the Clock: Music Television, Postmodernism, and Consumer Culture* (New York: Methuen, 1987).

Hugh Kenner, *The Mechanic Muse* (New York: Oxford University Press, 1987).

Derek Kidner, *The Wisdom of Proverbs, Job and Ecclesiastes: An Introduction to Wisdom Literature* (Downers Grove, IL: InterVarsity Press, 1985).

Meredith G. Kline, *Kingdom Prologue* (privately published by Dr. Kline, 1985-1986).

Richard Kostelanetz, ed., *The New American Arts* (New York: Collier Books, 1965).

Hilton Kramer, The Age of the Avant-Garde: An Art Chronicle of 1956-1972 (New York: Farrar, Straus and Giroux, 1973)

———, "The Art Scene of the '80s," *New Art Examiner*, October 1985, pp. 24-28.

———, "The Death of Andy Warhol," *The New Criterion*, May 1987, pp. 1-3.

———, "The 'Primitivism' Conundrum," *The New Criterion*, December 1984, pp. 1-7.

———, *The Revenge of the Philistines: Art and Culture, 1972-1984* (New York: The Free Press, 1985).

Abraham Kuyper, *Lectures on Calvinism* (Grand Rapids: Eerdmans, 1931).

Christopher Lasch, *The Culture of Narcissism: American Life in an Age of Diminishing Expectations* (New York: Warner Books, 1979).

Stephen R. Lawhead, *Turn Back the Night: A Christian Response to Popular Culture* (Westchester, IL: Crossway Books, 1985).

Clive Staples Lewis, *The Abolition of Man, or Reflections on Education with Special Reference to the Teaching of English in the Upper Forms of Schools* (New York: Macmillan, 1947).

———, ed., *Essays Presented to Charles Williams* (Grand Rapids: Eerdmans, 1966).

———, *An Experiment in Criticism* (New York: Cambridge University Press, 1961).

———, *Of Other Worlds: Essays and Stories* (New York: Harcourt Brace Jovanovich, 1966).

———, *They Asked for a Paper: Papers and Addresses* (London: Geoffrey Bles, 1962).

———, *The Weight of Glory and Other Addresses*, revised and expanded edition (New York: Macmillan, 1980).

Lucy Lippard, *Pop Art* (New York: Thames and Hudson, 1966, 1967, 1970).

Dwight Macdonald, *Against the American Grain* (New York: Random House, 1962).

Jerry Mander, *Four Arguments for the Elimination of Television* (New York: Quill, 1978).

David Marc, *Demographic Vistas: Television in American Culture* (Philadelphia: University of Pennsylvania Press, 1984).

David Marc, "Understanding Television," *The Atlantic*, August 1984, pp. 33-44.

Greil Marcus, *Lipstick Traces: A Secret History of the Twentieth Century* (Cambridge: Harvard University Press, 1989).

———, *Mystery Train: Images of America in Rock 'n' Roll Music*, second edition (New York: Dutton, 1982).

Jacques Maritain, *Creative Intuition in Art and Poetry* (Princeton: Princeton University Press, 1953).

George M. Marsden, ed., *Evangelicalism and Modern America* (Grand Rapids, MI: Eerdmans, 1984).

———, *Fundamentalism and American Culture: The Shaping of Twentieth Century Evangelicalism, 1870-1925* (New York: Oxford University Press, 1980).

Gerald Mast, *A Short History of the Movies*, second edition (Indianapolis: Bobbs-Merrill, 1976).

Allen J. Matusow, *The Unraveling of America: A History of Liberalism in the 1960s* (New York: Harper & Row, 1984).

John S. Mbiti, *African Religions and Philosophy* (Garden City, NY: Anchor Books, 1969).

Marshall McLuhan, *Understanding Media: The Extensions of Man* (New York: New American Library, 1964).

Richard Meltzer, *The Aesthetics of Rock*, new Foreword by Richard Meltzer, new Introduction by Greil Marcus (New York: Da Capo Press, 1970, 1987).

Joshua Meyrowitz, *No Sense of Place: The Impact of Electronic Media on Social Behavior* (New York: Oxford University Press, 1985).

James Miller, *"Democracy Is in the Streets": From Port Huron to the Siege of Chicago* (New York: Simon and Schuster, 1987).

Mark Crispin Miller, *Boxed In: The Culture of TV* (Evanston: Northwestern University Press, 1988).

James Monaco, *Celebrity: The Media as Image Makers* (New York: Delta Books, 1978).

——, *How to Read a Film: The Art, Technology, Language, History and Theory of Film and Media* (New York: Oxford University Press, 1977).

——, *Media Culture* (New York: Delta Books, 1978).

Michael Novak, *The Joy of Sports: End Zones, Bases, Baskets, Balls, and the Consecration of the American Spirit* (New York: Basic Books, 1976).

William L. O'Neill, *Coming Apart: An Informal History of America in the 1960s* (New York: Times Books, 1971).

Robert Pattison, *The Triumph of Vulgarity: Rock Music in the Mirror of Romanticism* (New York: Oxford University Press, 1987).

Neil Postman, *Amusing Ourselves to Death: Public Discourse in the Age of Show Business* (New York: Viking, 1985).

Ted Prescott, "Let's Get Primitive," *Eternity*, September 1985, pp. 21-26.

Charles A. Reich, *The Greening of America* (New York: Random House, 1970).

Eric Rhode, *A History of the Cinema: From Its Origins to 1970* (New York: Hill and Wang, 1976).

H. R. Rookmaaker, *Art Needs No Justification* (Downers Grove, IL: InterVarsity Press, 1978).

——, *The Creative Gift: Essays on Art and the Christian Life* (Westchester, IL: Crossway Books, 1981).

——, *Modern Art and the Death of a Culture* (Downers Grove, IL: InterVarsity Press, 1970).

Bernard Rosenberg, David Manning White, eds., *Mass Culture: The Popular Arts in America* (Glencoe, IL: The Free Press, 1957).

Harold Rosenberg, *Art and Other Serious Matters* (Chicago: University of Chicago Press, 1985).

—, *The Tradition of the New* (Chicago: University of Chicago Press, 1960).

Paul Rudnick, Kurt Andersen, "The Irony Epidemic," *Spy*, March 1989, pp. 92-98.

Leland Ryken, *The Christian Imagination: Essays on Literature and the Arts* (Grand Rapids: Baker Book House, 1981).

—, *Culture in Christian Perspective: A Door to Understanding and Enjoying the Arts* (Portland: Multnomah Press, 1986).

—, *Windows to the World: Literature in Christian Perspective* (Grand Rapids, MI: Zondervan, 1985).

Dorothy L. Sayers, *The Mind of the Maker* (Cleveland: Meridian Books, 1941).

Herbert Schlossberg, *Idols for Destruction: Christian Faith and its Confrontation with American Society* (Nashville: Thomas Nelson, 1983).

Quentin Schultze, *Television: Manna from Hollywood?* (Grand Rapids: Zondervan, 1986).

Tony Schwartz, *Media: The Second God* (New York: Random House, 1981).

—, *The Responsive Chord* (Garden City, NY: Anchor Books, 1973).

Tom Shales, "The Re Decade," *Esquire*, March 1986, pp. 67-72.

Roger W. Shattuck, *The Banquet Years: The Origins of the Avant-garde in France, 1885 to World War I*, revised edition (New York: Vintage Books, 1968, 1955).

Edward Shils, "Daydreams and Nightmares: Reflections on the Criticism of Mass Culture," *Sewanee Review*, 65 (1957), pp. 587-608.

Susan Sontag, *A Susan Sontag Reader*, Introduction by Elizabeth Hardwick (New York: Farrar, Straus, Giroux, 1982).

Nikos Stangos, ed., *Concepts of Modern Art*, revised edition (New York: Thames and Hudson, 1981).

Ben Stein, *The View from Sunset Boulevard: America as Brought to You by the People Who Make Television* (New York: Basic Books, 1979).

John R. W. Stott, *Your Mind Matters: The Place of the Mind in the Christian Life* (Downers Grove, IL: InterVarsity Press, 1972).

Wladyslaw Tatarkiewicz, "The Great Theory of Beauty and Its Decline," *The Journal of Aesthetics and Art Criticism*, Winter 1972, pp. 165-180.

Nick Thimmesch, ed., *Aliteracy: People Who Can Read But Won't* (Washington, DC: American Enterprise Institute, 1984).

Keith Thomas, *Man and the Natural World: A History of the Modern Sensibility* (New York: Pantheon Books, 1983).

Robert Farris Thompson, *Flash of the Spirit: African and Afro-American Art and Philosophy* (New York: Random House, 1983).

Calvin Tomkins, *Off the Wall: Robert Rauschenberg and the Art World of Our Time* (New York: Penguin, 1980).

Michael Ventura, "Hear That Long Snake Moan," *Whole Earth Review*, Spring 1987, pp. 28-43; Summer 1987, pp. 82-91.

Geerhardus Vos, *Biblical Theology: Old and New Testaments* (Grand Rapids: Eerdmans, 1948).

Richard M. Weaver, *Ideas Have Consequences* (Chicago: University of Chicago Press, 1948).

David Manning White, ed., *Pop Culture in America* (Chicago: Quadrangle Books, 1970).

Marie Winn, *The Plug-In Drug: Television, Children, and the Family*, revised edition (New York: Penguin Books, 1985).

Tom Wolfe, *The Painted Word* (New York: Bantam Books, 1975).

Nicholas Wolterstorff, *Art in Action: Toward a Christian Aesthetic* (Grand Rapids: Eerdmans, 1980).

——, *Until Justice and Peace Embrace* (Grand Rapids: Eerdmans, 1983).

Richard Saul Wurman, *Information Anxiety* (New York: Doubleday, 1989).

NOTES

CHAPTER ONE *Of the World, But Not in the World*

1. (Westchester: Crossway Books, 1985).
2. "Evangelicalism as a Democratic Movement," in *Evangelicalism and Modern America*, ed. George Marsden (Grand Rapids, MI: Eerdmans, 1984), pp. 71-82.
3. *Ibid.*, p. 79ff.

CHAPTER TWO *What Is Culture, That Thou Art Mindful of It?*

1. "Learning in War-Time," in *The Weight of Glory and Other Addresses*, revised and expanded edition (New York: Macmillan, 1980), p. 20.
2. *Ibid.*
3. *Ibid.*, p. 21.
4. *Ibid.*, p. 23ff.
5. Published with "The Idea of a Christian Society" in a single volume entitled *Christianity and Culture* (New York: Harcourt Brace Jovanovich, 1968).
6. *Ibid.*, p. 100.
7. *Ibid.*
8. "The Idea of a Christian Society," p. 37.
9. "Notes," p. 90ff.
10. (New York: Simon and Schuster, 1987).
11. *Ibid*, p. 39.
12. "Notes," p. 91.
13. *Ibid.*
14. *Ibid.*, p. 92.
15. *Ibid.*
16. *The Wisdom of Proverbs, Job & Ecclesiastes* (Downers Grove, IL: InterVarsity Press, 1985), p. 11.
17. *Ibid.*, p. 12.

CHAPTER THREE Would You Take Jesus to See This Planet?

1. *Kingdom Prologue*, Volume 1 (privately published, 1986), p. 55.
2. *Ibid.*, p. 58.
3. *Ibid.*, p. 58ff.
4. *Biblical Theology: Old and New Testaments* (Grand Rapids, MI: Eerdmans, 1948), p. 42.
5. Kline, *Kingdom Prologue*, Volume 2 (privately published, 1985), p. 14.
6. *Ibid.*, Volume 1, p. 105.
7. *Ibid.*, p. 105ff.
8. Nicholas Wolterstorff, *Until Justice and Peace Embrace* (Grand Rapids, MI: Eerdmans, 1983), p. 19.

CHAPTER FOUR Popular Culture and the Restless Ones

1. "Historical Perspectives of Popular Culture," contained in *Mass Culture: The Popular Arts in America*, eds. Bernard Rosenberg and David Manning White (Glencoe, IL: The Free Press, 1957), p. 47.
2. Franklin L. Baumer, *Modern European Thought: Continuity and Change in Ideas, 1600-1950* (New York: Macmillan, 1977), p. 68.
3. Quoted in Lowenthal, p. 47.
4. *Ibid.*, p. 48.
5. Many critics, especially in the 1930s, 1940s, and 1950s, used the terms "popular culture," "mass culture," and "kitsch" virtually interchangeably. "Mass culture" is a useful term because it isolates what is really distinctive about popular culture: that it is mass-produced. Shakespeare can be (and has been) popular, but his work, even if written for the masses, was not mass-produced. "Kitsch," a loanword from German, literally means "trash." Art critics often prefer this term, since it focuses attention on aesthetic norms rather than on the sociological status of popular culture. In one important essay, Dwight Macdonald even refused to use "mass culture" and called it "Masscult," because it had virtually nothing to do with culture in the more rarefied sense. I will generally use "popular culture" because it has become the most accepted term.
6. Dwight Macdonald, "A Theory of Mass Culture," in Rosenberg and White, *Mass Culture*, p. 60.
7. See especially Berger's *The Capitalist Revolution: Fifty Propositions about Prosperity, Equality, and Liberty* (New York: Basic Books, 1986).
8. See Robert Hughes's *The Shock of the New* (New York: Alfred A. Knopf, 1980) for a lively discussion of the interaction between new technology and the birth of modernism in the visual arts. A similar if much more focused story is told about machines and modernism as they influenced literature by Hugh Kenner in *The Mechanic Muse* (New York: Oxford University Press, 1987).
9. *All That Is Solid Melts into Air: The Experience of Modernity* (New York: Simon and Schuster, 1982), p. 345.
10. "Avant-Garde and Kitsch," originally published in 1939, republished in *Art and Culture: Critical Essays* (Boston: Beacon Press, 1961), p. 10.
11. "Liberalism and the Religion of Art," in *Critical Questions: On Music and Letters, Culture and Biography, 1940-1980* (Chicago: University of Chicago Press, 1982), p. 175.

12. "Of Happiness and of Despair We Have No Measure," in Rosenberg and White, Mass Culture, p. 505.
13. Popular Culture and High Culture: An Analysis and Evaluation of Taste (New York: Basic Books, 1974), p. 59.
14. Ibid.
15. Op. cit., p. 534ff.
16. Ibid., p. 535.
17. "A Theory of Mass Culture," p. 70.
18. The Cultural Contradictions of Capitalism (New York: Basic Books, 1976, 1978), p. 34.
19. "De Descriptione Temporum," in They Asked for a Paper: Papers and Addresses (London: Geoffrey Bles, 1962), p. 21.
20. The Image, or What Happened to the American Dream (New York: Atheneum, 1961), p. 9.
21. From The Collected Poems and Plays, 1909-1950 (New York: Harcourt, Brace & World, 1971).
22. The Cultural Contradictions of Capitalism, p. 21.
23. "Avant-Garde and Kitsch," p. 10.
24. "Liberalism and the Religion of Art," p. 170.
25. "Of Happiness and of Despair We Have No Measure," p. 529.

CHAPTER FIVE Accounting for Taste

1. These titles are not taken from actual articles, but they are fully in the spirit of such periodicals.
2. Ellen K. Coughlin, "In Face of Growing Success and Conservatives' Attacks, Cultural-Studies Scholars Ponder Future Directions," Chronicle of Higher Education, January 18, 1989, p. A-4ff.
3. Alexis de Tocqueville, Democracy in America, trans. George Lawrence, ed. J. P. Mayer (Garden City, NY: Anchor Books, 1969), p. 247.
4. Against the American Grain (New York: Random House, 1962), p. 404.
5. The Aesthetics of the Popular Arts," Journal of Aesthetics and Art Criticism, Spring 1966, p. 353.
6. Ibid., p. 354.
7. Ibid.
8. Ibid.
9. Ibid.
10. Ibid., p. 356.
11. Ibid., p. 357.
12. Ibid., p. 358.
13. Ibid.
14. Ibid.
15. Dwight Macdonald similarly observes that a work of popular culture "is necessarily at a distance from the individual since it is specifically designed to affect not what differentiates him from everybody else — that is what is of liveliest interest to him — but rather to work on the reflexes he shares with everybody else"(Against the American Grain, p. 24ff.).
16. "The Aesthetics," p. 355
17. Against the American Grain, p. 25. See also Chapter 2, "From Hero to

Celebrity: The Human Pseudo-Event," in Daniel Boorstin's *The Image, or Whatever Happened to the American Dream* (New York: Atheneum, 1961). Boorstin's discussion of celebrityism, while dated, is extremely helpful, as are many of his insights on our culture's "extravagant expectations."

18. *Op. cit.*, p. 359.
19. *Ibid.*
20. "On Fairy-Stories," in *Essays Presented to Charles Williams*, ed. C. S. Lewis (Grand Rapids, MI: Eerdmans, 1966), p. 76. See also C. S. Lewis, "On Stories," in *Of Other Worlds: Essays and Stories*, ed. Walter Hooper (New York: Harcourt Brace Jovanovich, 1966), pp. 3-21.
21. *Op. cit.*, p. 361.

CHAPTER SIX *Better to Receive*

1. (Cambridge University Press, 1961).
2. *Ibid.*, p. 1.
3. *Ibid.*, p. 2.
4. *Ibid.*, p. 2ff.
5. *Ibid.*, p. 3.
6. *Ibid.*
7. *Ibid.*, p. 88.
8. *Ibid.*, p. 19.
9. *Ibid.*, p. 19ff.
10. *Ibid.*, p. 113ff.
11. *Ibid.*, p. 85ff.
12. *Ibid.*, p. 125ff.
13. "Avant-Garde and Kitsch," p. 14.
14. *Op. cit.*, p. 126.
15. *Ibid.*, p. 137.
16. *Ibid.*, p. 138.
17. A friend recently remarked that so much of the music sung in evangelical churches today (influenced as it is by pop music) has such a triteness about it that "children aren't learning any songs they can sing at funerals." For more on popular music's limited emotional "palette," see Chapter 9.

CHAPTER SEVEN *Before the Revolution*

1. Discussed by Gilbert Seldes in "The People and the Arts," in Bernard Rosenberg and David Manning White, *Mass Culture in America* (Glencoe, IL: The Free Press, 1957), p. 89ff. This article was originally written in 1951. Although Seldes is generally very positive about popular culture, he is very upset about the degeneracy of comic books. One wonders whether he would be as sympathetic to today's popular culture.
2. Cited in James Miller, *"Democracy Is in the Streets": From Port Huron to the Siege of Chicago* (New York: Touchstone Books, 1987), p. 315.
3. (New York: Times Books, 1971), p. 200.
4. Cited in Dore Ashton, *American Art Since 1945* (New York: Oxford University Press, 1982), p. 147.
5. "The Death of Andy Warhol," *The New Criterion*, May 1987, p. 2ff.

6. Joseph Epstein, "It's Only Culture," *Commentary*, November 1983, p. 60.
7. *Ibid.*, p. 57.
8. "Liberalism and the Religion of Art," p. 171.
9. Roger Shattuck, *The Banquet Years: The Origins of the Avant-Garde in France, 1885 to World War I*, revised edition (New York: Vintage Books, 1968), pp. 29-42.
10. *Ibid.*, p. 37.
11. (New York: Knopf, 1980, p. xv).
12. Cited in Malcolm Bradbury and James McFarlane, eds., *Modernism, 1890-1930* (New York: Penguin Books, 1976), p. 20.
13. "*De Descriptione Temporum,*" in *They Asked for a Paper: Papers and Addresses* (London: Geoffrey Bles, 1962), p. 14.
14. *Ibid.*, p. 20.
15. *Ibid.*, p. 18ff.
16. Malcolm Bradbury and James McFarlane, eds., *Modernism, 1890-1930*, p. 27.
17. *The Cultural Contradictions of Capitalism*, p. xxii.
18. Cited in Paul Johnson, *Modern Times: The World from the Twenties to the Eighties* (New York: Harper & Row, 1983), p. 8.
19. Cited by Sarah Whitfield in an article on Fauvism in *Concepts of Modern Art*, revised edition, ed. Mikos Stangos (New York: Thames and Hudson, 1981), p. 16.
20. *The Cultural Contradictions of Capitalism*, p. xxi.
21. *Ibid.*
22. "Avant-Garde and Kitsch," p. 4.
23. *Has Modernism Failed?* (New York: Thames and Hudson, 1984), p. 14.
24. *Op. cit.*, p. 6.
25. *Ibid.*, p. 7.
26. *Ibid.*, p. 8.
27. "The Age of the Avant-Garde," in *The Age of the Avant-Garde: An Art Chronicle of 1956-1972* (New York: Farrar, Straus and Giroux, 1973), p. 7.

CHAPTER EIGHT *Where Have All the Standards Gone?*

1. Clive Staples Lewis, *An Experiment in Criticism* (Cambridge: Cambridge University Press, 1961), p. 8ff.
2. *Ibid.*, p. 9.
3. Calvin Tomkins, *Off the Wall: Robert Rauschenberg and the Art World of Our Time* (New York: Penguin Books, 1980), p. 163ff.
4. *The Cultural Contradictions of Capitalism*, p. 121.
5. *Ibid.*, p. 120ff.
6. *On Moral Fiction* (New York: Basic Books, 1978), p. 126.
7. *Critical Questions: On Music and Letters, Culture and Biography, 1940-1980*, p. 175.
8. "Art, Technology, and Nietzsche," *Journal of Aesthetics and Art Criticism*, Fall 1973, p. 98ff.
9. "The Age of the Avant-Garde," in *The Age of the Avant-Garde: An Art Chronicle of 1956-1972* (New York: Farrar, Straus and Giroux, 1972), p. 7.

10. Cited in Bertram Jessup, "Crisis in the Fine Arts Today," *The Journal of Aesthetics and Art Criticism*, Fall 1970, p. 5.
11. "The American Action Painters," in *The Tradition of the New* (Chicago: University of Chicago Press, 1960), p. 25.
12. Richard Kostelanetz, "A Conversation with Robert Rauschenberg, *Partisan Review*, Winter 1968, cited in Bertram Jessup, "Crisis in the Fine Arts Today," p. 6.
13. *The New York Times*, March 17, 1968, cited in *ibid.*, p. 6.
14. *The Cultural Contradictions of Capitalism*, p. 133.
15. "The Development of British Pop," in Lucy R. Lippard's *Pop Art* (London: Thames and Hudson, 1970), p. 32.
16. *Ibid.*, p. 36.
17. Cited in Lucy Lippard, *Pop Art*, p. 86. Lichtenstein may have been less than honest here. Critic Robert Hughes has said that "Lichtenstein's avowed intention in the early sixties was to paint a picture so ugly nobody would hang it" (*The Shock of the New* [New York: Knopf, 1981], p. 351).
18. Cited in Hughes, *op. cit.*, p. 344.
19. Op cit.., p. 11.
20. *Ibid.*, p. 82.
21. *American Art Since 1945* (New York: Oxford University Press, 1982), p. 121.
22. *The Shock of the New*, p. 364.

CHAPTER NINE Popular Culture's Idiom: Rock Around the Clock

1. Ned Rorem, *Music and People* (New York: George Brazillier, 1968), p. 10.
2. Simon Frith and Howard Horne, *Art into Pop* (London: Methuen, 1987), p. 73. Frith and Horne's entire book is a study of the interplay between the art schools and rock culture.
3. (New York: Simon and Schuster, 1987), p. 69.
4. Cited by Robert Pattison in *The Triumph of Vulgarity: Rock Music in the Mirror of Romanticism* (New York: Oxford University Press), p. 9. The study he refers to is reported by Claire V. Wilson and Leona S. Aiken, "The Effect of Intensity Levels upon Physiological and Subjective Affective Response to Rock Music," *Journal of Musical Therapy* 14:2 (1977), p. 62n.
5. Cited in Mary Harron, "McRock: Pop as a Commodity," in Simon Frith's anthology, *Facing the Music* (New York: Pantheon Books, 1988), p. 186.
6. (New York: Random House, 1970), p. 225.
7. *Ibid.*, p. 226.
8. *Ibid.*, p. 245.
9. Quoted in Daniel Bell, *Cultural Contradictions*, p. 17.
10. *Critical Questions: On Music and Letters, Culture and Biography, 1940-1980* (Chicago: University of Chicago Press, 1982), p. 171.
11. Franklin L. Baumer, *Modern European Thought: Continuity and Change in Ideas, 1600-1950* (New York: Macmillan, 1977), p. 270ff.
12. *Ibid.*, p. 271.

13. *Ibid.*, p. 274.
14. *Ibid.*, p. 278.
15. (New York: Oxford University Press, 1987).
16. *Ibid.*, p. xi.
17. *Ibid.*
18. Ted Prescott, "Let's Get Primitive," *Eternity*, September 1985, p. 22.
19. Robert Pattison, *The Triumph of Vulgarity*, p. 141.
20. Robert Hughes, *The Shock of the New* (New York: Knopf, 1981), p. 128.
21. *Ibid.*
22. *Op. cit.*, p. 39.
23. Reprinted as "Hear That Long Snake Moan," in two parts, *Whole Earth Review*, Spring 1987, pp. 28-43, and Summer 1987, pp. 82-92.
24. *Ibid.*, Part I, p. 31.
25. *Ibid.*
26. *Ibid.*, p. 36.
27. *Ibid.*, Part II, p. 89.
28. *African Rhythm and African Sensibility: Aesthetics and Social Action in African Musical Idioms* (Chicago: University of Chicago Press, 1979), p. 141.
29. *Op. cit.*, p. 64.
30. Pascal Bruckner, *The Tears of the White Man: Compassion as Contempt* (New York: Macmillan, 1986), p. 66. Bruckner's entire book critiques "Third-Worldism," showing how much ostensible compassion is really a form of exploitation, involving the projection of virtues onto primitive peoples, the massaging of guilt, and other fantasies that have nothing to do with actually helping people in need.
31. *Op. cit.*, p. 26.
32. *Ibid.*, p. 67.
33. *Ibid.*, p. 68.
34. *Ibid.*, p. 90.
35. "Rock 'n' Roll High School," *End of the Century* (Sire, 1980).
36. "School Days," *The Great Twenty-Eight* (Chess, 1957, 1982).
37. *Op cit.*, p. 95.
38. *Breakfast in America* (A&M, 1979).
39. *Op. cit.*, p. 89.
40. Cited in Daniel Bell, *The Cultural Contradictions of Capitalism*, p. 143.
41. *Op cit.*, p. 111ff.
42. *Ibid.*, p. 186ff.

CHAPTER TEN *Popular Culture's Medium: The Entertainment Appliance*

1. Mark Crispin Miller, *Boxed In: The Culture of TV* (Evanston, IL: Northwestern University Press, 1988), p. 7.
2. *Ibid.*, p. 8.
3. *Ibid.*, p. 10.
4. Tony Schwartz, *Media: The Second God* (New York: Random House, 1981), pp. 3-9.
5. Jacques Ellul, *The Humiliation of the Word* (Grand Rapids, MI: Eerdmans, 1985), p. 116.

6. Miller, *Boxed In*, p. 17.
7. See Tony Schwartz, *The Responsive Chord* (Garden City, NY: Anchor Books, 1973), pp. 18-22.
8. *Ibid.*, pp. 24ff. It should be noted that Schwartz is not just a media hack; he has produced commercials for over four hundred corporations and products and has worked on media campaigns for two presidential campaigns and hundreds of candidates at other levels of government. He is not principally a theorist, but a very sophisticated practitioner explaining his craft.
9. Ellul, *The Humiliation of the Word*, p. 184ff.
10. *Ibid.*, p. 186.
11. *Ibid.*, p. 187. It should be noted that in the articles on the relationship between rock 'n' roll, discussed in Chapter 7, Michael Ventura notes that Voodoo and Catholicism seem to have gotten along rather well in native habitats (Haiti, New Orleans), but Protestantism (which he clearly hates with a passion) has never accommodated Voodoo. (Part I, p. 36). The mind/body split Ventura despises seems to be more prominent in Protestant than in Catholic theology and practice.
12. *Ibid.*, p. 187ff.
13. *The Responsive Chord*, p. 118.
14. *Ibid.*
15. Martin Esslin, *The Age of Television* (San Francisco: W. H. Freeman and Co., 1982), p. 6.
16. *Ibid.*, p. 8.
17. *Amusing Ourselves to Death* (New York: Viking, 1985), pp. vii, viii.
18. *Op. cit.*, p. 22.
19. *Ibid.*
20. (New York: Oxford University Press, 1985).
21. Meyrowitz also discusses how television blurs the difference between childhood and adulthood, between male and female, and between those in authority and those under authority.
22. Tom Shales, "The Re Decade," *Esquire*, March 1986, p. 68.
23. *Ibid.*, p. 67.
24. *Ibid.*, p. 68.
25. Umberto Eco, *Postscript to the Name of the Rose* (San Diego: Harcourt Brace Jovanovich, 1984), p. 67ff.
26. *Op. cit.*, p. 72.
27. Mark Crispin Miller, "Deride and Conquer," in Todd Gitlin, ed., *Watching Television* (New York: Pantheon, 1986), p. 184.
28. *Ibid.*
29. Robert Hughes, *The Shock of the New*, p. 345.
30. *Op. cit*, p. 110.

CHAPTER ELEVEN *Where Do We Go from Here?*

1. Jacques Ellul, *The Humiliation of the Word*, p. 268.
2. *Ibid.*
3. Robert Pattison, *The Triumph of Vulgarity*, p. 186.
4. This is a line on the cover of Stephen R. Lawhead's *Turn Back the Night: A Christian Response to Popular Culture* (Westchester, IL: Crossway

Books, 1985), which provides some insightful advice about being wise consumers of popular culture. Quentin Schultze's *Television: Manna from Hollywood?* (Grand Rapids: Zondervan, 1986) is another recent study that focuses on prudent television-watching.

5. I recommend Marie Winn's provocative *The Plug-In Drug: Television, Children, and the Family* (New York: Penguin Books, 1977) as helpful reading for parents. But don't wait to read it until your kids are watching programs you don't like. Their addiction is too advanced by then. I would also strongly recommend that parents read Neil Postman's *Amusing Ourselves to Death* (New York: Viking, 1985). It is not directed at parents, but it is the best single book available on the social and cultural effects of television.

I N D E X